CW01185384

Joyce Mansour

In the Glittering Maw: Selected Poems

translated from French by C. Francis Fisher

with a preface by Mary Ann Caws

WORLD POETRY

In the Glittering Maw: Selected Poems by Joyce Mansour
Copyright © Cyrille Mansour, 2024
English translation copyright © C. Francis Fisher, 2024
Preface copyright © Mary Ann Caws, 2024

First Edition, First Printing, 2024
ISBN 978-1-954218-21-5

World Poetry Books
New York, NY
www.worldpoetrybooks.com

Distributed in the US by SPD/Small Press Distribution
www.spdbooks.org

Distributed in the UK and Europe by Turnaround Publisher Services
www.turnaround-uk.com

Library of Congress Control Number: 2024930184

Cover art: Pierre Alechinsky, "Braises," 1977, lithograph.
Image courtesy of the artist and Galerie Lelong & Co., Paris.

Cover design by Andrew Bourne
Typesetting by Don't Look Now
Printed in Lithuania by BALTO Print

World Poetry Books publishes exceptional translations of poetry from a broad range of languages and traditions, bringing the work of modern masters, emerging voices, and pioneering innovators from around the world to English-language readers in affordable trade editions. Founded in 2017, World Poetry Books is a 501(c)(3) nonprofit and charitable organization based in New York City and affiliated with the Translation Program and the Humanities Institute at the University of Connecticut (Storrs).

UCONN
HUMANITIES INSTITUTE

Table of Contents

Mansour's Violence of Vision

JOYCE PATRICIA ADÈS WAS BORN to a wealthy family of Syrian-Jewish descent in a hamlet in the Scottish Borderlands. The family didn't stay long in England and Joyce grew up in Cairo, Egypt, speaking English and Ladino at home. When she was 19, Joyce married Henri Naggar, but he died of cancer just six months after their wedding. She married an older man, the Cairene banker Samir Mansour, the next year. With Samir, she perfected her French—he refused to speak anything else. Together, they frequented literary salons in Cairo, where she was exposed to Surrealism through local luminaries like Georges Henein (one of the founders of the group Art and Liberty), who among other literary allies, helped circulate her work at home and abroad. In 1953, she published her first book, *Cris* (Screams), with the Parisian publisher Éditions Seghers.

This life in Cairo would not last. In 1952, Gamal Abdel Nasser led the Egyptian revolution against King Farouk, with whom the Mansours socialized. By 1954, most of their family's assets in Egypt had been seized by the government. The couple moved to Paris as exiles, never to return.

In Paris, the Surrealist atmosphere galvanized Mansour's energies and enthusiasms. André Breton, an early champion of her work, became a close friend—they spent afternoons together touring flea markets and exchanging ideas. A passionate lover of mythologies and a practitioner of rituals, Mansour developed a poetry alive to the language and drama of ceremonies, and an enthusiasm conducive to the magic of images and excess. It was in Mansour's famed Parisian salon, on December 2, 1959, at ten at night, that *The Execution of the Last Testament of the Marquis de Sade* took place to celebrate the anniversary of the great Sade's death. Canadian artist Jean Benoît appeared in a ten-foot-high, blood-splattered costume with feathers at the crotch, wearing a mask of four superimposed heads and a stomach in the form of an egg, on crutches and accompanied by blaring horns, screeching sounds, and stomach howlings.

Mansour is a many-voiced writer, remarkably and multiply bizarre. The chameleon seems to preside over these poems, which shift both topics and temporalities. Full of suggestive, purposeful omissions, her poems are as subtle as they are enormously erotic. In her late poems, of which the present volume is a substantial and representative selection, excess spurts out from accented visions full of far-out colors and ecstatic gestures, fascinating and over-the-top. Here Mansour gives free rein to a violence of vision.

What grabs me in C. Francis Fisher's translation of Mansour's later poems is a set of detailed moves that reveal the translator's sensitivity to the reverberations of language in the smallest spaces. Take these lines from the poem "You Abandon Me Nightly," for instance:

> Dans la mare profonde où tremble mon visage
> Glissant comme des pleurs sur le malaise qu'était hier
>
> In this deep pond where my face trembles
> Slippery like tears on yesterday's malaise

Here, rather than render the verb *glissant* as "slipping" or "sliding," Fisher moves toward an adjective to convey the wider feeling of "slippery." Though a literal-minded critic might object, "slippery" covers more space, the kind of anti-critical risk worth taking.

You can feel the translator's reveling in the words confronting each other in "The Chameleon's Tongue," taking a joyful plunge into such sounds and implied sights of "la gueule étincelante"—"the glittering maw." Fisher has discovered a certain surety and speed of decision-making, which, in these pages of Mansour, merits our trust.

As someone accustomed, in an old-fashioned mode, to critical nitpicking, I can scarcely fail to delight in the final poem's directive:

> Better to be shortsighted than clairvoyant
> In a world of little rodents

There is of course nothing little in this truly important poet, and this translation is no nibble at Mansour's production: this is a gulp worth gulping.

—Mary Ann Caws

In the Glittering Maw

from *Birds of Prey*

(*Rapaces*, 1960)

La cuirasse

Quand la guerre pleuvra sur la houle et sur les plages
J'irai à sa rencontre armée de mon visage
Coiffée d'un lourd sanglot
Je m'étendrai à plat ventre
Sur l'aile d'un bombardier
Et j'attendrai
Quand le ciment brûlera sur les trottoirs
Je suivrai l'itinéraire des bombes parmi les grimaces de
  la foule
Je me collerai aux décombres
Comme une touffe de poils sur un nu
Mon œil escortera les contours allongés de la désolation
Des morts brasillants de soleil et de sang
Se tairont à mes côtés
Des infirmières gantées de peau
Pataugeront dans le doux liquide de la vie humaine
Et les moribonds flamberont
Comme des châteaux de paille
Les colonnades s'enliseront
Les astres bêleront
Même les pantalons de flanelle s'engloutiront
Sans l'espace géant de la peur
Et je rincerai les dents découvertes violette d'extase
  dithyrambique
Hystérique généreuse
Quand la guerre pleuvra sur la houle et sur les plages
J'irai à sa rencontre armée de mon visage
Coiffée d'un lourd sanglot

The Breastplate

When war begins to rain on the swell and on the beaches
I will go to meet it armed with my face
Coiffed with a heavy sob
I will lie flat on my stomach
Atop the wing of a bomber
And I will wait
When the cement begins burning the sidewalks
I will follow the bombs' routes amidst the grimaces of the
    crowd
I will stick to the rubble
Like a tuft of hair on a nude
My eye will escort the stretched contours of desolation
The dead blazing with sun and blood
Will be silent by my side
Nurses gloved in skin
Will wade in the soft liquid of human life
And the dying will burn
Like castles of straw
The colonnades will sink
The stars will bleat
Even woolen slacks will vanish
Without the giant space of fear
And I'll rinse my bare teeth purple with dithyrambic ecstasy
Generous hysterics
When war begins to rain on the swell and on the beaches
I will go to meet it armed with my face
Coiffed with a heavy sob

Règle de vie

Manger un œil dans un œuf
Un cheval ou un cerf
Un cerveau mou santé
Un basset un violon
Manger pour manger
S'étrangler de chair
Agiter son anus sur un fanal de vair
Manger pour mourir dans un sanglot de sang
Se nourrir pour empêcher les autres
De vous manger

Rule of Life

Eat an eye in an egg
A horse or a deer
A healthy soft brain
A hound a violin
Eat for eating's sake
Choke on flesh
Shake its anus on a leather lantern
Eat to expire in a blubber of blood
Feed to keep others
From eating you

Le repoussoir

Bourrelées de honte
Branlantes sur leurs jambes de boie
Deux femmes aux yeux de folles
Relevèrent leurs jupes leurs jupons leurs antennes
Et se caresserènt la cuisse
Le mollet le genou
L'instant de la virginité s'était échappé
Et derrière le paravent
L'infirmière faisait la moue

The Foil

Racked with shame
Rickety on their stiff legs
The moment virginity escaped
Two women with crazed eyes
Raised their skirts their petticoats their antennae
And caressed their thighs
The calf the knee
And behind the curtain
The nurse sulked

Biographie

Les brumes savantes des feuillages d'automne
Le lilas les lubies le thé des nurses anglaises
Le désert qui se trémousse derrière le paravent
Le frère qu'on épouse
L'aïeul qu'on enterre
L'enfant qui perd ses dents
Le cobra qu'on caresse
Et qui sourit
Les meurtres de velours et de crème
Les chuchotements musicaux des
Nous à genoux
Les parents qui sommeillent dans la grande poche de la nuit
Soupirs de lait gifles aux ailes de fer bouches sceptiques
    dilemmes
La mort du mari qui ne marche pas encore
Les montagnes aux hoquets de neige qui approchent et qui
    s'éloignent
Avec chaque lettre mal épelée de l'enfant qui implore
Et qui se balance entre les feuilles transies de sa treizième
    année
Sûre de son pouvoir et du lever de l'amour
Sûre de son pouvoir
Et de l'inépuisable mort

Biography

The wise mists of autumn foliage
The lilacs the whims the tea of English nurses
The desert that wriggles behind the screen
The brother we marry
The grandfather we bury
The child that loses their teeth
The cobra we caress
And who smiles
The murders of velvet and cream
The musical whispers
Of us on our knees
The parents who sleep in the canyon of night
Milky sighs iron-winged slaps doubting mouths dilemmas
The death of the husband who does not walk yet
The mountains with hiccups of snow approaching and receding
With each misspelled letter of the child who begs
And who balances between the frozen leaves and their
        thirteenth year
Sure of their power and the rise of love
Sure of their power
And tireless death

Les yeux des amis

Je cherchais ton cœur sous un monceau de débris
Un étrange parfum hirsute et prévoyant
Fouillait à mes côtés sans éteindre son cigare gris
Des plats réchauffés passaient sous mon nez
Des ligules de lamas des plumes de lilas
Des tentacules qui lient plus étroitement qu'une maladie
Des souvenirs non comestibles des gravures de nus aux
hanches rebondies
Des étages du passé grignoté par la démence
D'autres plus conformistes fardés de poudre de riz
Cernaient leurs meubles de pompe et de dentelles de cérémonie
Je cherchais ton cœur sous un monceau de papiers gras
Mais le parfum de ton amour a éteint son cigare sur le tapis
Et je suis restée seule avec les cendres d'une savante plaisanterie

Friends' Eyes

I was looking for your heart beneath a pile of debris
A strange perfume shaggy and prudent
Was frisking by my side without putting out its gray cigar
Warmed-up leftovers passed under my nose
Ligules of llamas feathers of lilac
Tentacles that bind more tightly than disease
Inedible memories of naked engravings with full hips
Floors of the past eaten away by dementia
Others more conformist painted with rice powder
Surrounded their furniture with pomp and ceremonial lace
I was looking for your heart under a pile of gray papers
But the perfume of your love put out its cigar on the carpet
And I was left alone with the ashes of a clever joke

from *White Square*

(*Carré Blanc*, 1965)

La porte de la nuit est fermée à clef

Retrouver le désert
Mon pays desséché et secret
La vie la vie même
L'enchanteur endormi dans les mirages vert profonde
Du tapis
Traverser la Judée le frais Jardin clos
Le cimetière
Ô vent de Galilée miroitement de la nostalgie
Sous une lune de pierre
Fuir les tigrures des nuages sur le sol aveuglant
Fuir en dansant
Un vent plaintif s'est levé dans mon cœur
De pâles paroles tombées des tuiles ruissellent sur ma peau sèche
(Mer morte du souvenir au creux de l'après-midi)
Viens enlace-moi
Allons vers les forêts
Les ravins
Les blancs pommiers
Je rêve consumée par une folie dangereuse
L'horizon brûlant et impie
Fait signe
Et des pyramides s'érigent
Sur la plaque tournante
De midi
Je rêve ou je rêve sans espoir de retour
Seul l'aveugle sait maudire la bougie échevelée
Les tendres yeux étirés de l'amour sont cailloux pour toi
Bijoux trous tanières
Luxure et putréfaction
Coutures et balafres de l'église
Nommée
Or

Night's Door Is Locked

Find the desert
My scorched and secret country
Life life itself
The sleeping enchanter in deep green mirages
Of carpet
Cross Judea the cold enclosed garden
The cemetery
O wind of Galilee shimmering nostalgia
Beneath a stone moon
Flee the stripes of clouds on the blinding ground
Flee while dancing
A doleful wind rises in my heart
Pale words fallen from tiles stream over my dry skin
(Dead ocean of memory in afternoon's hollow)
Come encircle me
Let us go to the forest
The ravines
The white apple trees
I dream consumed with a dangerous madness
The burning and godless horizon
Beckons
And pyramids rise
On the turntable
Of noon
I dream yes I dream without hoping to return
Only the blind know how to curse the disheveled candle
The tender eyes of love are pebbles for you
Jewels holes lairs
Luxury and putrefaction
Clothes and seams of the church
Named
Gold

Tu m'as abandonnée nuitamment

Mes heures coulent impassibles
Au fond du miroir moucheté de bronze
Des nuages font la parade
Dans la mare profonde où tremble mon visage
Glissant comme des pleurs sur le malaise qu'était hier
Des feuilles frissonnent sur le treillis du souvenir
Frissonnent et tourbillonnent et pourtant restent immobiles
Quelque part au fond de moi un moule se cristallise.

You Abandon Me Nightly

My hours flow impassively
At the bottom of the mirror speckled with bronze
Clouds parade by
In this deep pond where my face trembles
Slippery like tears on yesterday's malaise
Leaves shudder on the trellis of memory
Shudder and whirl and yet stand still
Somewhere in my depths a mold crystallizes

Fragment d'un appel

Ma bouche va et vient
Entre le téléphone et le toit
Voyages ciselés
Par d'étranges boucles brunes
Veines variqueuses d'un très vieux bois
Que vous écrire
Les longs périples
Du demi-sommeil
Les passages ondoyants
Du moindre de mes gestes
Mes phrases mal tournées dans leurs souliers de satin
Trébuchent dans les méandres du sentier
Exsangue du Grand Tétanos
Quelle heure peut-il être
Collée aux cloisons de l'attente
Je t'écoute
Et quelque part dans le lointain
Un ivrogne nommé Devoir
Vomit

Fragment of a Call

My mouth comes and goes
Between the telephone and the roof
Travels chiseled
By strange brown curls
Varicose veins of very old wood
What to write to you
The long journeys
Of half-sleep
The undulating passages
Of my slightest gestures
My misconstrued phrases in their satin shoes
Stumble in the twists and turns of the path
Bloodless from the Grand Tetanus
What time can it be
Glued to the waiting room
I listen to you
And somewhere in the future
A drunkard named Duty
Vomits

Quels sont ces couteaux qui brillent au-dessus de la seine

Le soleil mordu
Par un bel animal
N'est plus qu'agonie
Et fuite devant
La faim
Faim aussi que ce ventre bombé
Sous le manteau noir de la bête
Sommeil
Aucune science ne m'apporte
Une fin aisée sur ta couche mobile
Ma rageuse passion écorche le gazon
Le sourire de ta mère illumine mon visage
Voilà la pierre qui crèvera ton orgueil
Quant à moi sans chaleur à qui ferai-je ma cour

What Are These Knives That Shine Above the Seine

The sun bitten
By a beautiful animal
Is nothing but agony
And flees before
Hunger
Hungry as this bloated belly
Beneath the black coat of the beast
Sleep
No science can bring me
An easy end on your moving bed
My raging passion flays the grass
Your mother's smile lights up my face
This is the rock that will crush your pride
But whom will I court without heat

Sous la tour centrale

pour Matta

Des mains erraient sur les touches
Et des paroles étranges venant d'Elle
Flottaient à la surface du ruisseau
J'écoutais le dialecte des sexes qu'on déshabille
Des mains écrivaient sur les vannes
Vingt-quatre heure sur vingt-quatre
Et des assassinats devaient suivre
Dans le même crépuscule bleuâtre où sifflent les serpents
d'acier
Où crient les mouettes et s'épanouissent les femmes mûres
Aux pistils enflâmes et blessures de pacotille
J'étais un peu intimidée
Ç'aurait été tellement délicieux
De pouvoir uriner dans la rue

Beneath the Central Tower

for Matta

Hands wandered over the keys
And strange words issued from Her
Floated on the surface of the stream
I heard the dialect of undressing sexes
Hands wrote on the valves
Twenty-four seven
And assassinations would have to follow
In the same bluish twilight where the steel serpents hiss
Where seagulls cry and mature women flourish
With inflamed pistils and junky wounds
I was a little intimidated
It would have been so luxurious
To have the power to piss in the street

Lorsque Myriam sortit de l'extase

Je suis de retour
Fini les vendanges
Les oreilles jaunes du matin
Se dressent contre la porte
Irritants problèmes
De patine
Fini la cueillette des olives
Sur les collines de l'adultère
Fini les jouissances passives
Je ne saurai combattre la narcose
Endormie comme la boue des jardins emmurés
Mon sexe resplendit de la grande soif amère
L'exquis bâillement de la mort
Pourquoi sais-je triste sans le savoir
Sans noyau de nèfle gonflé de sang rustique
À tenir ainsi qu'un dernier de veuve
Entre mes doigts abreuvés de lumière
Comment satisfaire ma manie de fraîcheur
Aucune passion
Aucun vieux châtiment
Qui ne porte l'uniforme du vice
Je tombe sur le sol aux grands mouvements marins
Et tourbillons de paves aux sonores accents
De tambour
Je tombe et je remonte et la surface de la ville
Ne peut être loin dans la misère et dans le temps
Je suis revenue trop tôt
Ô fils de ma maternelle flamme
Salut

When Miriam Emerges from Ecstasy

I'm back
Harvest is over
The yellow ears of morning
Stand against the door
Irritating problems
Of patina
No more picking olives
On the hills of adultery
No more passive pleasures
I can't fight narcosis
Asleep like mud in enclosed gardens
My sex gleams with a great bitter thirst
The exquisite yawn of death
Why do I know sadness without understanding it
Without the medlar pit swollen with rustic blood
To be held like a widow's last
Between my fingers drenched in light
How to satisfy my craze for freshness
No passion
No old punishment
That does not wear vice's uniform
I fall to the ground with great sealike movements
And swirls of cobblestones with the sound
Of drums
I fall and I rise and the surface of the city
Cannot be far from misery and time
I came back too soon
O son of my maternal flame
Hello

Crème fraîche

Ma mère me mange
Me torture
Et pour m'empêcher de la suivre
Elle m'enterre
Je mange ma famille
Je crache sur leur debris
Je hais leurs maladies funambulesques
Et leurs hallucinations de l'ouïe
Prenez garde au dentifrice
Qui blanchit sans détruire
Mieux vaut s'égayer en dévorant les siens
Que de marcher à quatre pattes
Boire
Ou essayer de plaire
Aux filles

Crème Fraîche

My mother mauls me
Tortures me
And to keep me from following
She buries me
I eat my family
I spit on their remains
I detest their fear of heights
And auditory hallucinations
Beware of toothpaste
Whitening without destruction
Better to indulge in eating your kin
Than to crawl around
Drinking
Or try to please
The daughters

Régions barbares

Mon lit file à travers champs chambres et crépuscules
Aux vertes promesses d'orages et logiques embouteillages
Je perds pied entre les draps
Sucée par la fange
Silencieuse entêtée comme l'enfant que l'on appelle
Et quo l'on sait n'être
Plus là
Blême comme la souffrance de la seule femme au monde
Debout dans le petit jour
Il passe

Je ne veux pas vivre sans toi
Voilà tout

Barbaric Regions

My bed spins across fields rooms and dusks
To the green promises of storms and logical congestion
I lose my footing between the sheets
Sucked in by the mire
Silent stubborn like the child we call
And know is not
There anymore
Pale like the suffering of the only woman in the world
Standing at dawn
He passes

I don't want to live without you
That is all

La piste du brouillard

De désespoir
Je mangerai la terre
Demain
Le grand chien noir
Obscurcit la lampe
Partie la violette sombre aux pommettes spatulées
Partie l'étoile oisive des plaines gonflées de pluie
L'abeille cherche l'épingle au tréfonds de mon régard
Midi
Ma pupille éclat sur la berge
L'arc-en-ciel de l'orgasme se reflète au plafond
Sous tes genoux serrés mon œil
S'ossifie
Dans ton sommeil oblique
Une végétation d'étain
Prend feu
Et puis c'est toute l'orbite
Qui se vide dans ma main
Pourquoi ne prendrais-je pas une virgule pour un cœur
La rue n'est que masturbation
Du femme

The Trace of Fog

Of despair
I will eat the earth
Tomorrow
The big black dog
Obscures the lamp
Gone the dark violet with razed cheekbones
Gone the idle star from rain-swollen plains
The bee seeks a pin in the depth of my gaze
Noon
My pupil bursts on the bank
The orgasm's rainbow reflects on the ceiling
Beneath your tight knees my eye
Ossifies
In your oblique sleep
Pewter vegetation
Ignites
And then it is the whole orbit
That empties into my hand
Why don't I take a comma for a heart
The street is only
Female masturbation

Jeudi froid

Arbre bleu
Perce-neige aux impossibilités d'écrire
L'inaccessible virgule qui précède le mot
Nuit
Riche sous ma chevelure
Je prie gravement
Je rêve
Une large bande d'ombre
Coupe
Ton visage de sa mauvaise certitude
La tristesse tombe au ralenti
Odeur de mégot
Ovaire inactif
Tango
Ma dépouille pose nue
Sans surcharge de chaînes
Ni vain désespoir
Il ne peut y avoir de cloison entre la neige et la nuit

Cold Thursday

Blue tree
Snowdrops with their inability to write
The inaccessible comma preceding the word
Night
Rich beneath my tresses
I pray gravely
I dream
A wide strip of shadow
Cuts
Your face from its grim certainty
Sadness falls in slow motion
Cigarette butt odor
Lazy ovary
Tango
My hide poses naked
Free from the extra weight of chains
And vain despair
There can be no division between snow and night

La langue du caméléon

Je viendrai chez toi le quarantième jour
Je viendrai car mes membres blanchissent en ton absence
J'ai faim de tes ennemis
Honte de ma faiblesse aux mouvements de marée
Ondulante comme le serpent avide
Je frôlerais l'extase
Si je n'avais peur de cueillir les cendres
Dans le ventre de ma mère
Dans le creux de la houle
Dans la gueule étincelante
De l'église

The Chameleon's Tongue

I will come to your home on the fortieth day
I will come because my limbs whiten in your absence
I am hungry for your enemies
Ashamed of my weakness for tidal currents
Undulating like the greedy snake
I would rub against ecstasy
If I weren't afraid to gather the ashes
In my mother's womb
In the hollow of the swell
In the glittering maw
Of the church

Sans loquet ni caviar

Le sable brûlent sur la neige
Ta langue sur l'aisselle du chien
Toute chose arrive à tout homme
Il suffit d'attendre
Ma palme africaine sur le vacarme de la justice
Mon bas indigo entre les lèvres du muezzin
Détails laconiques
Plaques tournantes grattoirs
De loche
Monotonie et semence
Pourboires
Le soulagement du vieux chien
L'œil rivé sur le vide
Quand ta langue balafrée par mille nervures de corne
Arrêta sa démarche ô parodie
De procession
Pointilliste
Barrière
La mort avait signé au bas de son nombril
Mortification et prière

Without Latch or Caviar

Sand burns on the snow
Your tongue on the dog's armpit
Everything happens to every man
Just wait
My African palm on the din of justice
My indigo stocking between the muezzin's lips
Laconic details
Grating cogs
Of the loach
Monotony and seed
Tips
The old dog's relief
The eye fixed on the void
When your tongue scarred by thousands of raised horns
Stopped its march o parody
Of procession
Pointillist
Barrier
Death signed below his navel
Mortification and prayer

La nuit en forme de bison

Je pense trop souvent aux cérémonies funèbres
Saute petit poisson rouge
Je pense trop souvent aux tombeaux ravagés
Aux viellées oppressives
Je ne sais repousser la veuve ni adoucir son parchemin
Servante des cimetières depuis l'antiquité perdue
La terre est le toit de ma maison

Partout dans mes songes flotte une odeur féminine
Comme une plaie érotique aux aiguilles ultra-fines
Comme une ruine
Comment chasser les cadavres porteurs de contagion
Vaste assemblée en pyjamas orange

Et vitrines d'antiquaires
Comment sceller les catafalques sans toucher à la soupe
Comment épousseter un mort sans déranger ses paupières
Où irai-je quand *toutes* les routes seront surveillées

Bison Shaped Night

I think too often of funerals
Jump little goldfish
I think too often of ravaged tombs
Of the oppressive olden days
I do not know how to repel the widow nor soften her
parchment
That cemetery servant since lost antiquity
The earth is the roof of my house

A feminine odor floats over my dreams
Like an erotic wound with ultra-fine needles
Like a ruin
How to hunt corpses carrying contagion
Large gathering in orange pajamas

And the windows of antique shops
How to seal the caskets without touching the soup
How to dust a dead body without disturbing the eyelids
Where will I go when *all* roads are watched

Bronze comme la nuit tombée

Hier le rose pastel
Colorait mes rêves encore
Tout embués de vous
Le grand glaïeul
Bramait sur ses ergots
Vingt bustes de mortes
Aux langues lourdes
Et haleine stagnante
Opprimante venaison de l'aube
Pressaient leurs lèvres blêmes
Sur l'encolure fantomale
De ton nom
Hier le velours verdoyait
Sous les ponts
Le goût des vieux arbres
M'obsède
La mer siffle sur le sol battu
J'ai peur d'être seule
Sang et vomissure de la vie réelle
Je construirai des sexes à secret
Des cauchemars héréditaires
Poussiéreuses fleurs d'automne
J'ai peur d'être seule dans la tombe

Bronze Like Nightfall

Yesterday pastel pink
Colored my dreams again
Everything clouded with you
The huge gladiolus
Roaring on its spurs
Twenty busts of dead women
With heavy tongues
And stagnant breath
Oppressive venison of dawn
Pressed their pale lips
On the ghostly neckline
Of your name
Yesterday the velvet was green
Under the bridges
The taste of old trees
Obsesses me
The sea whistles on the beaten ground
I am afraid of being alone
Blood and vomit of real life
I will build sexes in secret
Hereditary nightmares
Dusty autumn flowers
I'm afraid of being alone in the grave

from *The Damnations*

(*Les damnations*, 1967)

Le désir du désir sans fin

Je te croyais roux
Bouc lippu de ma tendresse
Indifférente
Matière gommeuse aux lignes fuyantes
Et arides couchants d'opium
Le froid augmente dans la clairière
Mes poumons refleurissent
D'un sanglot flamboyant
Plus glacé qu'une gravure
Plus sérieux qu'un hélleniste
Au Panthéon
Tu m'observes
Et quelque chose de dominateur
Pétrit mon épiderme de ses volontés convulsives

J'ai ouvert mes bras
Ma grande plaie saline
Sous la passerelle de l'hiver
Et aussitôt l'objet remua
Craintivement dans sa cage
Et le violoncelle tapi
Dans l'oreille triste de l'escalier
À la manière d'une flèche brisée
Dans une bouteille d'encre de Chine
Hoqueta une note teintée
Ô industrieuse Isis
De souffrances orientales

Serai-je un jour déçue
Le vent renouvellera-t-il
L'herbe pure du canapé
Saurai-je flotter sans baromètre

Desire for Endless Desire

I thought you were red
Full-lipped goatee of my indifferent
Tenderness
Gummy material with receding and arid lines
Opium sunsets
Cold builds in the clearing
My lungs bloom again
With a fiery sob
Icier than intaglio
More serious than a Hellenist
At the Pantheon
You watch me
And something dominant
Kneads my skin with its convulsive wills

I opened my arms
My great saline wound
Beneath winter's bridge
And right away the object stirred
Fearfully in its cage
And the cello lurking
In the sad ear of the staircase
Like a broken quill
In a bottle of India ink
Which hiccupped a stained note
O industrious Isis
Of oriental suffering

Will I someday be disappointed
Will the wind refresh
The pure grass of the couch
Can I float without a barometer

Ni flasque pylône
Autour des jarres de crépuscule
Serai-je un jour ruisseau
Quand tout en toi crie : feu
Il m'est difficile de penser à la mort
Quand sur mon ventre hésitent de grands oiseaux
Aux pâles retards de sperme
Et habilités d'écume

Je ne saurais suivre la trame
Des tortures mythologiques
Ni dénombrer les gémissements
Des coléoptères de salon
Quand sur l'épaule de la tumultueuse girafe
Ta chemise viendra cracher son ombre

Je ne crains pas la colère des chambres secrètes
Ni la mâchoire féconde de l'armée carnassière
Aucun homme avec moi ne place son pied
Sur la pente calcinée de la haine
L'arbre immergé passe aux sons de l'enjôleuse cithare
Je me vengerai de ta racine aux narines empourprées
La Veuve Noire fermera ses lèvres de pierre
Sur ta grande nervosité
Chaste et trouée de sommeil

Tu ne sauras m'échapper

Qui connaît le profil de ma voluptueuse rosace
Plus frénétique encore
Que l'anémone frileuse
Elle trempe sa tige étroite
Dans l'onde de l'autre Seine
Pourquoi mes doigts portent-ils

Or a flaccid pylon
Amid dusk's jars
Will I ever be a creek
When everything in you screams: fire
It is hard for me to think of death
When large birds hesitate on my stomach
With slow pale sperm
And foamy capacities

I can't follow the plot
Of mythological tortures
Nor count the wails
Of beetles
When on the shoulder of the tumultuous giraffe
Your shirt will spit its shadow

I do not fear the anger of secret rooms
Nor the fecund jaw of the carnivorous army
No man of mine places his foot
On the charred slope of hatred
The submerged tree moves to the sounds of the bewitching
        zither
I will avenge myself on your root with flared nostrils
The black widow will close her lips of stone
On your great nervousness
Chaste and holey with sleep

You cannot escape me

Who knows the profile of my voluptuous rosette
Even more frenetic
Than the skittish anemone
She soaks her narrow stem
In the wave of the other Seine

De petites têtes de mort à leurs douces extrémités
Ces brûlants serpents aux onglées exquises
Flattent ton orgueil sans jamais en démordre

Que de calamités sous les tréteaux de la banquise
Étirée comme l'horizon dans un hublot de fourmilière
Défenestrée comme lui
J'enjambe ta bouche
Ta balustrade
J'étale
Ma lourde frisure
En filigrane
Sur la cascade de ta vigne
Ici un lapin passait naguère
Sa vie errante souple et flottante
Sur le candélabre de l'inaction
Aux sept branches de supplices
Et aux homélies anciennes
Sauvez-moi cria-t-il du haut de sa passion
Personne n'entendit le brûlot amarante

Ta bouche se montre vorace de jouissances enfantines

Tu te souviens des monts velus de l'Angleterre
De ses figures de boue
Piquées
Au flanc de la semaine
Comme des mots proclamés trop fort
Trop fort
Dans le vent envenimé de la tombe
Il y a des morts qui respirent dans la profusion tropicale
D'avant-hier
Des mères comme la mienne
Qui toujours des anniversaires

Why do my fingers wear
Little skulls on their soft tips
Those burning snakes with exquisite nails
Flatter your pride without bending it

What calamities under the trestles of ice
Stretched out like the horizon in the opening of an anthill
Defenestrated like him
I straddle your mouth
Your balustrade
I spread
My heavy golden curls
On the waterfall of your vine
Here a rabbit passed not long ago
His wandering life supple and suspended
On the candelabra of inaction
With seven branches of torture
And ancient homilies
Save me he cried at the height of his passion
No one heard the amaranth fire

Your mouth is voracious with childish pleasures

You remember the hairy hills of England
Its mud figures
Pricked
Flanking the week
Like words proclaimed
Too loudly
In the venomous wind of the grave
The dead who breathe in tropical profusion
Of the day before yesterday
Mothers like mine
Who always remember

Se souviennent
Beaux et clairs présents
Cheveux et dents salés
Mamelles concaves
Tristes échos de cimetière
J'attends oui j'attends
Me croyant délivrée
Des notes musicales assoiffées de paperasse
De ces yeux de basilic
Dans leur pagode de verre
Qui cuvent des cauchemars sous leurs jupons noirâtres
Et qui crient
Est-ce bien nécessaire
Sur une carte de visite
De jurer la fidélité
Quand le temps dans sa niche
Fait l'école buissonnière
Je sais que sous le pont
Tes yeux fous se sont noyé
Notre-Dame entrebâille ses savantes cuisses gothiques
Plus puissantes et plus fières
Qu'échafauds et belladones
Elles enferment ton roux visage
Dans le losange de vendredi
Je vois
Un petit lit de fer
Aux tentures douceâtres
Et volutes de léproserie
Un vaste choix de boursouflures
Sur ta poitrine incrustée
De joyaux exclusifs
Je sens ton sexe gouache de parfums
Féroce cache-pot de porcelaine
Plonger dans ma rétine

Birthdays
Beautiful and bright presents
Salty hair and teeth
Concave nipples
Sad cemetery echoes
I am waiting yes I am waiting
Believing myself delivered
From music thirsty for paperwork
From those basilisk eyes
In their glass pagoda
Who sleep off their nightmares under black petticoats
And who bellow
Is it really necessary
To swear loyalty
On a business card
When time in its niche
Skips school
I know that under the bridge
Your crazy eyes have drowned
Notre Dame parts her knowing gothic thighs
More powerful and more proud
Than scaffolds and nightshades
They tighten around your red face
In the diamond of Friday
I see
A small iron bed
With sweet curtains
And swirls of leprosy
Huge swaths of blisters
On your encrusted chest
Exclusive jewels
I smell your sex painted with perfume
Fierce porcelain planter
Diving into my retina

Éclats et arrachements du spasme vaginal
Il faut empêcher le pendu
D'avaler sa langue
Je sens sur mon coccyx
Un battement douloureux
Je voudrais couler pensive
Dans la blanche crème de tes artères
Glisser ma main nue sur l'échine moite de ta corolle
Mater ta plante cuivrée aux barbares cornets de neige
Je suis le tourbillon de Gomorrhe.

Splintering and tearing of the vaginal spasm
We must thwart the hangman
Swallow his tongue
I feel a pain throb
In my tailbone
I would like to sink pensively
Into the white cream of your arteries
To slide my naked hand along the moist spine of your corolla
To tame your coppery plant with barbarous snow cones
I am the maelstrom of Gomorrah

666

Au tournant d'un long rêve
De marbre à midi ô sourire de la Grèce
J'ai vu passer les mirages purpurins
Aux lents aveux mouillés
Et ondulations de la reine
Je t'attendais sûrement
Pauvre baudruche du désert
Et l'ennui horizontal de juillet
Taillait des figures naïves
Dans ma colère aux rideaux de tulle
Et fenêtres aveugles sur l'enfer
Il n'y a pas de clous
Pas de poussière
Dans l'anus d'une femme amoureuse
Et pourtant
J'ai vu mourir le Bélier sous la douce pluie lavande
Du Poisson-volant
J'ai vu osciller la mince silhouette du fracas
Sur la crête surannée
D'une verge
Verge sans perruque ni cascade
Verge faite comme moi
Pour attendre
Je voudrais pouvoir écrire
Ma joie sur la houille blanche
Des lettres d'amour tendre
Brouter à toute heure l'herbe sereine
Qui grésille autour de ta bouche
Aux bâillements de cuir et hectares boisés
De fumée rapide
Je voudrais savoir étaler des mots jaunes et verts
Sur le seuil du palais qui surplombe mon enfance

666

At the turn of a long dream
Of marble at noon O Greek smile
I saw orange mirages pass
To the slow wet confessions
And undulations of the queen
I doubtless waiting for you
Poor desert balloon
And the horizontal boredom of July
Naïve carved figures
In my anger with tulle curtains
And blind windows to hell
There are no nails
No dust
In the anus of a woman in love
And yet
I saw Aries die beneath the soft lavender rain
Of the flying fish
I saw the slender silhouette of the crash oscillate
On the quaint ridge
Of a penis
Penis without wig or waterfall
Penis made like me
To wait
I want to be able to write
My joy on white coal
Tender love letters
To graze anytime on serene grass
That sizzles around your mouth
With leather yawns and wooded hectares
Of swift smoke
I would like to know how to spread green and yellow words
On the threshold of the palace that overlooks my childhood

Faire perler ma vie
Ma vaillante banquise
Jusqu'à l'extrême pointe de ta grande frisure
En constellations de rubis
Il n'y a pas d'ivresse possible sous hypnose
Je sais comment nourrir le tourment
Le typhon le torrent la terrible giboulée
De Londres
Je connais le chiffre qui entoure les murs nus
De rides et de brassards
Plus bruyants que la bombe
Oui la bombe clinquante injure
Aux gratifications de pyramide
Forêts pervenches et griffonnages
A fleur
De guerre
Je suis le lion dans l'éblouissement de la pierre
Le jaune fourmillement du souci dans la pâteuse solitude
De Pompéi
La tricherie farouche de la multitude
Quand l'ombre de l'ombre de l'ombre
De mon immense ami
Passe
Rien n'est plus vrai que ta voix dans ces ruelles
Je l'écoute mieux à cheval
Face au téléphone sur son socle de parenthèses
À l'ogive suturée de la sultane
Je suis obéissante ainsi
Étendue à tes pieds comme une petite scène histoire
La foule a des appétits d'Etna
Te plairai-je un peu
Étirée sur mon miroir
Ainsi que l'isthme entre les deux Amériques
Mes cordes emmêlées

To make my life flow
My valiant icecap
To the extreme point of your great curl
In constellations of rubies
It is not possible to be drunk while hypnotized
I know how to feed torment
The typhoon the torrent the terribly sudden shower
Of London
I know the number that surrounds the bare walls
Of wrinkles and armbands
Louder than the bomb
Yes the flashy bomb insults
Pyramid gratifications
Periwinkle forests and scribblings
Flush
With war
I am the lion in the glare of the stone
The yellow swarming of concern in the pasty solitude
Of Pompeii
The multitude's fierce cheating
When the shadow of the shadow of the shadow
Of my immense friend
Passes
Nothing is truer than our voice in these passageways
I listen to it better on horseback
Facing the telephone on its pedestal of parentheses
To the sultan's sutured warhead
I am in this way obedient
Laying at your feet like a mythic little scene
The crowd has Etna's appetites
Will I please you a little
Stretched out on my mirror
As well as the isthmus between the two Americas
My tangled strings

Ma gorge nue
Haletante et morose je ne saurai te rejoindre
Le matin au lever du parc
Comment retrouver le vent flottant
De mes illusions perdues
Les cimes pluvieuses
Les stagnantes devantures
Ne reflètent plus que la trace des sangsues
Dans l'azur
Il paraît que le vertige des bouquets de très haute race
Le contact des langues sous le boisseau éolien
(En français dans le texte)
Effraient les crapauds nocturnes
Aux yeux bombés et clairs
Gobeurs de mouches et de merde
Tout le long des Champs-Élysées
Les dimanches sans télévision et jolie flûte champêtre
Les dimanches sans toi

Les trois cents éclatements ô parfums scandaleux
De mon pubis trahi pas ses loches
Les langues enjôleuses de ces serpents-insectes
Qui hantent ma toison une fois la pluie venue
Connaissent le supplice de la première pierre
Lancée à pleines mains sur la patinoire du rire
Elles tremblent et la ténébreuse figure
Enfouie
Dans ma floraison maudite
S'enfonce à tout jamais dans les sables mouvants du sexe
Quelle femme suis-je
Dis capricorne vil héraut de l'hiver
Pour combler les crevasses de l'attente toujours splendide
De ma passion couleur d'encens et de ma seule nudité
Ainsi je me lamente et crois te décevoir

My bare throat
Panting and morose I will not be able to reach you
Morning at sunrise in the park
How to find the floating wind
Of my lost illusions
The rainy peaks
The stagnant displays
Only reflect the trace of leeches
In the deep blue
It seems that the vertigo of bouquets of purebreds
The contact of tongues beneath the wind's bushel
(In French in the text)
Scares the nocturnal toads
With clear domed eyes
Guzzlers of flies and shit
All along the Champs-Élysées
Sundays without television and pretty country flutes
Sundays without you

The three hundred bursts O scandalous smells
Of my pubis betrayed by its breasts
The flirtatious tongues of these snake-insects
That haunt my fleece when the rains come
Knowing the torment of the first stone
Thrown with plenty of hands on the ice rink of laughter
They tremble and the shadowy figure
Buried
In my cursed bloom
Sink forever in the quicksand of sex
What woman am I
Say Capricorn vile herald of winter
To fill the cracks of my always splendid waiting
Of my incense-colored passion and my only nakedness
So I lament and think I'm disappointing you

Quand sur mon dos ton diamant rosâtre
Dérape
Il faut que je brûle
Mes perles en rang sur mes genoux
Que je m'arrache de ma chair
Ainsi qu'une lance peinte à fleur
De poitrine nue sous son blanc haubert
Il faut que je cherche sans rien abandonner
Le plaisir sans rides nu-pieds sur le gosier
Du bègue
Écoute
Ma chanson roule vers l'exil
Il faut que je vomisse
Dans l'air pur et la clarté
De ta bouche
Vois-tu les chalands qui charrient mon sang
À travers le tapis d'Éspagne
Vers Onan

Misères et croix de la croissance vigoureuse
Qui décrira le repas du soleil dans la maison de centaure
Qui fermera les yeux du document humain
Une fois l'abîme de verre étendu sur mes pupilles
Quel souffle animera les poumons du viaduc
Debout depuis mille ans sur la boule mouvante du mot
Midi
Oui quel doigt lourd abattra le portique
Sur le chaos de mes membres orgueilleusement raidis
Tels des gonfanons d'or sur une termitière

Les années en boue et en bois du Liban
Effaceront les traces des allées anciennes
De leurs résonnantes béquilles
Et leurs forts pieds carrés

When on my back your pinkish diamond
Skids
I must burn
My pearls in a row on my knees
I must tear myself from my flesh
Like a spear painted on the surface
Of a bare chest under a white hauberk
I must search without abandoning anything
The pleasure of wrinkleless feet on the neck
Of the stutterer
Listen
My song rolls toward exile
I have to vomit
In the pure air and clarity
Of your mouth
Do you see the barges that carry my blood
Through the Spanish carpet
To Onan

Miseries and crosses of vigorous growth
Who will describe the sun's meal in the house of the centaur
Who will close the eyes of the human document
Once the abyss of glass spread over my pupils
What breath will animate the lungs of the viaduct
Standing for a thousand years on the moving ball of the word
Noon
Yes what heavy finger will knock down the gate
On the chaos of my proudly stiffened limbs
Like golden bells on a termite mound

The muddy wooden years of Lebanon
Will blot out the traces of old alleyways
Of their resonant crutches
And their strong square feet

Les frémissantes traînées de verdure
Grimperont les marches aux broderies de genêts
Entre les imposantes statues aux sourires anémiques
Et les grands oiseaux ébréchés dans les sarments fluides
Rien ne restera de mon corps
La coupole de fumée s'élèvera à l'horizon
Triste d'être parjure en singeant le soleil
J'aurai froid
Je n'oserai appeler la sentinelle au petit jour
Ni frapper réellement sur le tambour du confesseur
L'échelle de soie se transforme en rétif balai
Je sais que je suis perdue
Pourtant je dédaigne les sacrifices sanglants
Je piétine dans la saumure
Ornée de toutes mes larmes
Et les dents étoilées de la triomphante Isis
Claironnent dans l'ordre dorique
De ces douze colonnes novices
De ma toute dernière nuit
L'angoisse hennit dans mes cheveux
Et un amour nouveau visse son visage sur le mien
L'heure n'est plus aux dolents à leurs pommeaux de cristal
Las est mon sein
Sans remords mon alezan
Qui vole vers la haute roche
De la paralysie Complète
Sur ses fins Sabots
D'or

Les fiers grains de mon collier
Loin de mon cou
S'éparpillent
Le lien est brisé entre la cœur et l'éclair
Demain est une grande plaque de sang

The quivering streaks of greenery
Will climb the broom-embroidered steps
Between imposing statues with anemic smiles
And the great chipped birds with spouts for mouths
Nothing will remain of my body
The dome of smoke will rise on the horizon
Sad to be perjured for aping the sun
I will be cold
I dare not call the sentry at dawn
Nor surely beat the confessor's drum
The silk ladder becomes a wayward broom
I know I am lost
Yet I despise blood sacrifices
I trample in the brine
Adorned with all my tears
And the starry teeth of triumphant Isis
Trumpet in the Doric order
Of these twelve novice columns
Of my very last night
Anguish whinnies in my hair
And a new love screws its face to mine
It is no longer time for the bereaved with their crystal knobs
Weary is my breast
Without remorse my chestnut
That flies toward the high rock
Of complete paralysis
On her fine hooves
Of gold

The proud beads of my necklace
Far from my neck
Scatter
The link is broken between the heart and lightning
Tomorrow is a large plaque of blood

Cosmos and Catastrophes

(*Astres et désastres*, 1969)

For P.A.

Sous le drap
Bouge
Le chaos
Dans le rire le hoquet
Freine
Trébuche et frappe encore
L'heureuse glotte acérée
La Sortie
La fumée lasse L'haleine vaginale
Le dernier souffle de pure peine
Éructe
Plaqué au sol par la pesanteur
D'un seul mot
Quand
Il y a des planches vides de tout désir
Des cheveux qui poussent sur des crânes ensevelis
Des sexes armés pour combattre
L'oubli
Le cerveau dans sa cage
Se croit lion libellule
Machine
Comment peut-on dormir une heure avant la grande nuit
Derrière
L'immense nuit du cri éternel
Il faut chanter la fièvre
La masturbation
Hurler la beauté de la chair
Jouir dans la bouche de la blanche sentinelle
Lévitations sans raideur
Anguilles
Il faut rire dans le vent L'écho
Accède au palier du souvenir vécu
Il faut manger le sexe de son père

Under the sheets
Chaos
Moves
In laughter hiccup
Stop
Stagger and strike again
The happy barbed glottis
The Exit
The tired smoke
The vaginal breath
The last gasp of pure pain
Belches
Pinned to the ground by the weight
Of a single word
When
There are boards empty of all desire
Hair growing on buried heads
Sexes armed to fight
Oblivion
The brain in its cage
Believes itself a dragonfly lion
Machine
How can you sleep a single hour before the big night
Behind
The immense night of the eternal cry
We must sing the fever
Masturbation
Roar the beauty of the flesh
Cum in the white sentinel's mouth
Floating without stiffening
Eels
We must laugh in the wind the echo
Reach the level of lived memory
We must eat our father's sex

Un homme est entré dans Palmyre
Sur le dos d'une petite cuillère
Il plana longtemps
Nébuleuse primitive
En crachant de la poussière lunaire

Un homme est entré dans sa mère
Sans ciller ni rendre son affreux baiser
Il perdit la raison entre ses cuisses de métal bleu
Et la lune se leva nue sur son père
Un homme est entré dans sa tête
Par l'orbite perforée du métro
Il s'aggloméra sans peine
À cet autre corps unique
La moule Marée haute des années vécues
Au plus bas de la nuit
Le sable se ride
La glacière s'allonge
Seul reste le sanglot
Chantre

Un homme
Nœud coulant
Pomme d'Adam
Chien errant Âme slave

Un homme a planté une rave fourchue
Dans l'œil laqué de son nombril
Au hasard
Puis accroupi comme un poisson
Dans sa gelée heureuse
Il féconda la terre
De sa mort

A man entered Palmyra
On the back of a little spoon
He hovered a long time
Primitive nebula
Spitting moon dust

A man entered his mother
Without blinking or returning her awful kiss
He lost his mind between her blue metal thighs
And the moon rose named over his father
A man entered his head
By the perforated orbit of the metro
He collected easily
Into this unique new body
The high-tide-mussel years lived
At the bottom of the night
The sand ripples
The glacier elongates
Only the sob remains
Cantor

A man
A noose
Adam's apple
Stray dog Slavic soul

A man planted a forked root
In the lacquered eye of his navel
At random
Then crouched like a fish
In his happy jelly
He fertilized the earth
With his death

Un homme déroba la langue priapique
Et la cacha derrière l'occiput
Astrologique
De la Vierge aux pupilles de cire
La guerre éclata dans don corsage ouvert
L'homme courut plus vite
Qu'une me
Déserte
Vers l'étoile qui saignait au loin
Si la haine sème la maladie
L'envie le cancer
Qui suspendra la rusée mandragore
Qui arrachera la pince du homard
Mort

Il y a une théorie du désert
Une musique une mélancolie
La mort migratrice fait des vagues sur le lac hostile
Elle nivelle les années d'écaille
Sur le ventre de la vieillesse-tortue
Son miroir encombré de joncs de marais
L'écorce battue de sa peau peinte
Les îles innombrables de son pubis ensablé
Tout en elle crie
peur
solitude
mensonge
Tout frissonne et rétrécit
L'aube se lève comme une très vieille femme
Le froid mépris de tes yeux une fois la nappe ôtée
Souligne que c'est fini
La mort commune
Passe

A man stole the phallic tongue
And hid it behind the astrological
Occiput
Of the virgin with waxen pupils
War broke out in her open bodice
The man ran faster
Than a deserted
Me
Toward the star that bled in the distance
If hatred sows disease
Envy cancer
That will suspend the cunning mandrake
That will tear the claw from the lobster
Dead

There is a theory of the desert
A music a melancholy
Migratory death makes waves on the hostile lake
It levels out the scaly years
On the old tortoise's stomach
Its mirror cluttered with reeds
The battered bark of her painted skin
The incomparable islands of her sandy pubis
Everything in her cries
fear
solitude
lies
Everything shivers and shrinks
The dawn rises like a very old woman
The cold contempt in your eyes once the tablecloth is removed
Makes clear that it is finished
Common death
Passes

from *Phallus and Mummy*

(*Phallus et momies*, 1969)

Phallus et momies

J'ai suivi la route parallèle
Derrière le tulle des ténèbres
Entre les cuisses de mes aïeux
Darde la langue hébraïque
L'art commence où le désir finit
Mate et sale
Sans haleine
Fasce d'argent sur champs de gueules
J'ai crevé dans ma peau
Ainsi qu'une enflure bleuâtre dans la boue
Saturne fait usage de son dard
Pour stimuler son appétit
La mort peut être nécessaire
Aux autres
Je hais les satisfaits
Les stériles les nantis
Un mort suit l'autre sans connaître son visage
Une femme traverse les rails
En sang en sang ensanglantée
Personne ne la voit personne dans
L'ascenseur
Le jaune insoutenable d'une voix de canari
Mélange d'arsenic et de colle
Relie les côtes aux barreaux et ne laisse point
D'espace pour l'oiseau
Tout casser
Briser l'image du pénis paternel
Lové comme un serpent dans un vase de Gallé
Écraser sa tête sous un talon d'acier
(Un vague sentiment de retour
Vagit dans le ravin

Phallus and Mummy

I followed the parallel road
Behind the tulle of darkness
Between the thighs of my ancestors
Darts the Hebrew language
Art begins where desire ends
Dull and dirty
Without breath
Silver strips on red fields
I died in my skin
Like a bluish swelling in the mud
Saturn uses his stinger
To stimulate his appetite
Death might be necessary
For others
I detest the satisfied
The sterile the wealthy
A dead man follows the other without knowing his face
A woman crosses the tracks
Bloody bloody oh so bloody
No one sees her there is no one
In the elevator
The unbearable song of a canary
Mixture of arsenic and glue
Bind the ribs to the bars and leave
No space for the bird
Break everything
Shatter the image of the paternal penis
Coiled like a snake in a Gallé vase
Crush his head under a metal heel
(A vague sense of return
Whimpers in the ravine

Passer outre)
Il faut rire en montant les marches de la vieille maison
Éventrer les acteurs égrenant leurs bigoteries
Haïr les fébriles égorger les assis
Déraciner les morts assoupis dans leurs excréments
Avaler cracher
Oublier maudire
La chair bêlante
Huileuse comme un lit défait
Il faut mastiquer éjaculer
Boucher les orifices
Replâtrer l'hymen
La mort est une porte-tambour
Un œuf saponaire un croupion
Il faut dégonfler le chancre sur la face divine
La détruire
Pissez fontaines
La vie hibernante des glaciers gonfle vos toisons de pierre
Vos clitoris s'écaillent
Ainsi que des crocodiles implantés dans le sable frais
Mort aux veules
Mort aux vrilles
Mort aux habitués de l'utérus
Mort aux isolés debout
Il y a du sparadrap sur la blessure de la vigne
Et une route parallèle à celle
Qui n'existe
Plus

Go on)
You must laugh while climbing the steps of the old house
Disembowel the actors shelling out their bigotries
Detest the feverish slit the throats of the seated
Uproot the dozing dead from their excrement
Swallow spit
Forget curse
The bleating flesh
Oily like an unmade bed
You must chew cum
Plug the orifices
Repair the hymen
Death is a revolving door
A soapwort egg a rump
You must lance the canker on the divine face
Destroy her
Piss fountains
The glacier's hibernating life swells your stone pelts
Your clitoris is flaking
Like crocodiles buried in the cold sand
Death to the trembling
Death to the tendrils
Death to the regulars of the womb
Death to those left standing
There is a bandage on the vine's wound
And a road parallel to that
Which no longer
Exists

Entre le rêve et la Révolte la raison vacille

Une phrase traverse la tête endormie
Il faut déjouer les tours de la cathédrale
Tours de sang dans le vent tournis
Brasillants tourniquets
Organes inexplorés
Abcès de fixation pour acrobates verbeux
L'araignée pendue à un cil
Guette son image dans l'iris du ciel
Un cheveu fictif remplace l'autre dans la soupière
Un cerveau respire mal sous le globe du souvenir
L'œil du cheval
Ne sachant où se poser
Revint à la charge
Explosion dans le flux vécu
Fixe les yeux Enflées les paupières
Lourds les miasmes dans le champ carnassier
Une phrase une seule phrase sur le mur creux de l'effroi
L'alun clarifie les eaux
Les notabilités de la gent boursière
Portent fièrement leurs croix de viande
Au revers de leurs insomnies
Ivre il faut vivre ivre
Écœurante équation du juste milieu
Entre les cuisses tièdes de l'homme rassis
Vit un rat
Il vomit
Triste fin pour un littérateur

Between Dream and Revolt Reason Vacillates

A sentence plagues the sleeping mind
You must outwit the cathedral towers
Towers of blood in the whirling wind
Glowing tourniquets
Unexplored organs
Abscess of fixation for verbose acrobats
The spider hung from an eyelash
A fake hair replaces the other in the tureen
A brain breathes shallowly beneath the globe of memory
The eye of the horse
Not knowing where to land
Returned to the load it carried
Explosion in the lived flow
Fix your eyes Swollen eyelids
Heavy the miasmas in the carnivorous field
A sentence a single sentence on the hollow wall of dread
Alum clarifies the waters
The famous stockbrokers
Proudly carry their crosses of meat
On the back of insomnia
Drunk one must live drunk
Disgusting equation of centrists
Between the tepid thighs of the stale man
Lives a rat
It vomits
Sad ends for a writer

La solitude tout court

Seconde Ève l'après-midi
Le soleil fond dans ses cheveux roux
Roux comme le flot de ses menstrues passes
(J'ai le sang à la tête)
Même décapité
Le phalène hérissé sur une flame
Lâche des œufs
Certains cuellent des oranges
Sous l'averse légère
D'autres ouvrent leurs cuisses
Éternuent
Ô vaste nuit frangée d'herbe
Priapique
La femme assise
Le clitoris debout
La langue s'est retirée
Le sang ne jaillit plus
Les femmes roussissent comme des feuilles
Blanchissent et se teignent
Ululent et métaphorent
Sur leur crochet hystérique
Ô vaste nuit bilingue comme une autopsie
Seconde Ève la nuit la nuit
Dans les coulées iodines du froid présent
Seule sur le sable battu

Simply Solitude

Second Eve in the afternoon
The sun melts in her red hair
Red like the flow of her previous menstruations
(I have blood on my mind)
Even decapitated
The moth bristled on the flame
Coward of eggs
Some pick oranges
Under the light shower
Others open their thighs
Sneeze
O vast night fringed with grass
Priapic
The seated woman
The standing clitoris
The tongue has retired
The blood no longer spurts
Women scorch like sheets of paper
Whiten and dye
Ululate and metamorphose
On their hysterical hook
O vast bilingual night like an autopsy
Second Eve the night the night
In the iodine flows of the present cold
Stranded on the battered sands

La femme de Loth

Pour A.J.

Il faut chasser la femme de Loth
Manger le pain sans sel
Sans larmes
Sans elle
Avide ouverte elle flambe
Empalée gluante sur le pied sec de l'ennui
Absente Attentive aux pulsations de sa vulve
elle
BAILLE
Dans le sens contraire de la violence érotique
La mort est contagieuse
Elle oriflamme debout
Le brasier de sang crépite
Autour de ses genoux
Il faut modeler les excréments
Lécher l'anus
Plonger sa figure dans l'amertume de la vieillesse
Faucher le blé qui fermente dans l'aisselle
Connaître l'offense La mort agitée de vers
La mort végétale rigide dans l'orgasme et le soubresaut
Tout sauf rien hurle la femme
Ne me laissez pas partir
Il faut chasser la femme de Loth
Il faut être *normal*

Lot's Wife

For A.J.

We must expel Lot's wife
Eat bread without salt
                                        Without tears
                                        Without her
Greedy open she flames
Sticky impaled on the dry foot of boredom
Absent Attentive to the throbbing of her vulva
                                                            she
                                                                YAWNS
Contrary to erotic violence
Death is contagious
She stakes her flag
A pot of blood crackles
Around her knees
We must mold the excrement
Lick the anus
Plunge the face into the bitterness of old age
Reap the wheat fermenting in the armpit
Know the breach that death combats
Rigid plant death in orgasm and shudder
Everything but nothing shouts the wife
Do not let me go
We must expel Lot's wife
We must be *normal*

from
To Signal the Machinist

(*Faire signe au machiniste*, 1977)

L'horizon de l'aveugle

Belzébuth
Paon moucheté
Aux érections jumelées
Aux éjaculations extrêmes
Tu fixes ton pénis à la roue du couchant
Dans l'axe du carcan
Famille
En moi la graine coloureuse rayonne
Le cri jaillit en gerbes
Tu jouis
J'aime l'été la poussière le blé hasardeux
Du désert
Que labourent le vent d'ouest et le bédouin géométrique
Sur son âne e
Au réveil
L'horreur recule le souffle inquiet
Le soleil à jamais se couchera
derrière les falaises
à dentition
sans pépites
Sur le rond d'osier d'une cervelle d'ammonite
Le jour où tu videras tes lombes
Dans la gorge d'une autre fille
Oui je suis jalouse
La solitude aux mains râpeuses pue la charogne
Le sable laissé à lui-même dérive dans le sens du soupir
La nuit creuse un trou
Au fond de l'impasse nommée douleur d'autrui
Et l'os de mes os

Horizon of the Blind

Beelzebub
Speckled peacock
With twin erections
With extreme ejaculations
You fix your penis to the sunset wheel
In line with the family
Straitjacket
In me the colorful seed shines
The cry gushes in wreaths
You cum
I love the summer the dust the hazardous wheat
Of the desert
That plows the west wind and the geometric bedouin
On his donkey
When he wakes
The horror sucks back the uneasy breath
The sun sets forever
          behind the toothless
                                        cliffs
                                             without gold
On the wickerwork of an ammonite brain
The day that you empty your loins
In the throat of another girl
Yes I am jealous
Rough-handed solitude reeks of the carcass
The sand left to its own devices drifts toward the sigh
The night digs a hole
At the depths of the impasse called pain of the others
And the bone of my bones

L'ombre gauchère de mon amour
Désir sans tendresse ni verbe à l'appui
Ma nuit ma vie même
Coule
Entre mes doigts
Entre mes cuisses
Sous les draps
Et le lit
Il vaut mieux étaler son beurre sur les tristes pavés
Du sommier
Que de tourner autour de son sexe Éternelle toupie
Aux orbes évasés en dentelles légères
Et spirales vagabondes

Un homme m'attend
En bas
Je glisse lisse et savonneuse
Entre deux rangées de palmiers
Et de couches de mortes
Vers sa bouche pour qui mon sexe plastronne
Crépite grince des dents et grésille
Sous mes pieds la complaisante banquise
Improvise
Il dort dans la chambre des aliments froids
La porte est murée
Le tapis grimpe le long des murs
Derrière le paravent un museau épanoui
Chuchote laisse-toi faire
Personne n'est normal dans le rêve d'autrui
Ainsi qu'une tache d'encre dans une paume impubère
Sans perdre quelques dents
Ô yeux ralentis de l'enfance soumise
Grincements craquements baisers embués
Taches de graisse sur le levain de la venimeuse

The left-handed shadow of my love
Desire without tenderness or verb in support
My night even my life
Flows
Between my fingers
Between my thighs
Under the sheets
And the bed
It is better to spread your butter on the sad cobblestones
Of the bed frame
Than to rotate around your eternally spinning sex
With splayed orbs in fine lace
And vagabond spirals

A man is waiting for me
Downstairs
I glide smooth and soapy
Between two rows of palm trees
And layers of dead
Toward his mouth for which my sex swells
Spatters gnashes and sizzles
Beneath my feet the complacent ice bank
Improvised
He sleeps in the cellar
The door is blocked
Carpet climbs the walls
Behind the screen a beaming muzzle
Whispers let yourself go
No one is normal in the dreams of another
Like an ink stain in a prepubescent palm
Without losing a few teeth
O slow moving eyes of obedient childhood
Squeaks creaks steamy kisses
Grease stains on the yeast of the venomous

Hostie
Comédies fausses sorties et mamelons élastiques
Quelques coups secs sur les doigts de la religion assise
Quelques tombes sous le sable errant
Même les ouvreuses de la fosse commune portent des
masques
Comment accompagner les accords du râle clandestin
Sinon par le cri
J'ai faim
Saurai-je engloutir l'outil émoussé
Saurai-je avaler la fade chlorophylle
Saurai-je abattre la main verte
Le pilier le palmier le poil la légende
Sans faire gicler la boue entre mes orteils écartés
Un homme m'attend dans le silence obscur
De sa tombe
Une huître flotte dans son chapeau mou
Son pénis est parti en costume d'escargot
Pour fuir il ne suffit point de lever les yeux
Fillette je dormais nue
Nue comme Jéricho
Une fois

Host
Fake exit comedies and elastic nipples
A few sharp blows on the fingers of seated religion
A few tombs under the restless sand
Even the diggers of mass graves wear masks
How else to accompany the last rites of the clandestine
 rattle
If not with a cry
I am hungry
Will I be able to devour the blunt tool
Will I be able to swallow the bland chlorophyll
Will I be able to chop down the green thumb
The pillar the palm tree the pelt the legend
Without squirting mud between my splayed toes
A man is waiting for me in the obscure silence
Of the tomb
An oyster floats in his limp hat
His penis fled in a snail costume
To flee is not enough to lift your eyes
Little girl I slept naked
Naked like Jericho
For once

Il y a des carrefours...

Il y a des carrefours où la nuit
La joie saute sur le dos
Du passant
Telle l'aube solitaire dans le vent acide
Le décapité meurt debout
Plus bas
Corps à corps dans la vase
Grouillante fournaise
Les vers
Fouets à triples lanières
Caressent la pointe des racines
De chair
Viande de sacrifice
Bijou de la putréfaction
Sans autre fardeau que ses bras
Noués coude à coude
Derrière
Gerbes de sang sur la terre promise
Prospectus d'engrais
Il y a des crachats au tréfonds du miroir
Des éraflures dans la neige
Des parjures croupissent
Dans les prunelles de nos compagnes
Buées et sueurs de la femme autoritaire
Nue sur le plancher
Vibrante de haine « Circulez » hurle
Évangeline
Trop tard
Le puits est tari les mouches parties

There Are Crossroads...

There are crossroads where at night
Joy jumps on the back
Of the passerby
Like lonely dawn in acid wind
The decapitated die standing
Lower
Body to body in the mud
Teeming furnace
The worms
Whips with three tails
Caress the tip of the roots
Of flesh
Sacrificial meat
Jewel of putrefaction
With no burden but his arms
Tied elbow to elbow
Behind
Sheaves of blood on the promised land
Fertilizer advertisement
There is spit in the depths of the mirror
Abrasions in the snow
Treachery languishing
In the pupils of our companions
Fogs and sweats of the authoritarian woman
Naked on the floor
Vibrating with hate "Get a move on"
Screams Evangeline
Too late
The well is dry the flies have left

Dans le fouillis de verdure
Un léger fumet d'aisselle hésite
Encore
Les jupons en écorce de phallus
Font office d'éteignoir
Soleil couchant
Il y a des cadavres vivants dans la bouche des
        nourrissons
Saule pleureurs
Des embryons enduits de cire mensongère
Dans l'aqueduc qui se déverse
Sur la plaine
Demain qui boira le sang de nos pères

In the jumble of greenery
A slight aroma of armpit lingers
Again
Petticoats in phallus bark
Act as an extinguisher
Sunset
There are living corpses in infants' mouths
Weeping willows
Embryos coated in fake wax
In the flowing aqueduct
On the plain
Tomorrow who will drink the blood of our fathers

Litanie pour un rêve prolongé

Dans les rues d'El Kantara sont méconnaissables au
crépuscule
Les peuples de la mort ont trente-neuf doigts d'ordure
Tressés sur leurs fronts
Couronnes de pères
Là-bas une tombe ressemble à un trottoir roulant
À l'envers
Les morts voyagent assis
Vers l'Est
Le désert
La poussière douce comme un ventre ouvert
La clarté d'une voix dorée sur tranche
La nuit édentée la savane
L'idée fixe d'étoile
Polaire
Le rire en rafale de la crécelle enfant
L'explosion ornementale de l'œil qui éclate
Sous la botte
L'épais jus de la corruption dans le vermeil colonial
L'église
Les empreintes digitales de la mort sont pâles et
privées de rayons
Le vent de midi se lève dans les cafés
Les yeux de ma mère égrènent un chapelet de testicules
Quelque part dans le forêt
Des pendus priapiques éternuent
Le scarabée enfouit sa boule sous la terre livide
L'hiver est prince d'olive

Litany for a Prolonged Dream

The streets of El Kantara are unrecognizable at dusk
The people of death have thirty-nine filthy fingers
Braided on their foreheads
Crowns of fathers
Over there a tomb looks like a moving walkway
In reverse
The dead travel sitting
To the East
The desert
The dust soft like an open stomach
The clarity of a golden voice on edge
The toothless night the savanna
The obsession of
The North Star
The gusty laughter of the child rattle
The ornamental explosion of the eye which bursts
Under the boot
The thick juice of corruption in colonial vermeil
The church
Death's fingerprints are pale and lack rays
The midday wind rises in the cafés
My mother's eyes count a rosary of testicles
Somewhere in the forest
Priapic hanged men sneeze
The scarab buries his ball beneath the livid earth
Winter is prince of olive

L'ombre de ma folie

Si je mange de la chair
Si je déchire tes paupières de mes mains
Si je mange le cerveau de mon ennemi
Vaincu
Si je piège mon pubis de rats aux dents cariées
Ce n'est pas pour me venger
Ma rivière est sans encombre
Ma forge surpeuplée d'artisans aveugles
Ne soufflait naguère que pour mieux attiser ta passion
Mes rêves ne tremblaient que dans les yeux des crocodiles
L'amour est l'issue close de l'hostie
Arrachés au sol
Maculés de boue et toujours
Gesticulant
Mes ennemis mon ennemi mon amant vont
Festoyant
Danser sur la tombe de mon ventre enseveli
Une passerelle de planches
Une palissade de troncs
Une forêt un œuf géant
Un arbre
Un mât aux voilures pesantes et plus basses
Que l'horizon vu de face quand la lune ne se retient plus
Tout bascule
Un mois un simple mois me sépare de cette autre
    verdure
Ma haine se divise en sanglots en gouttelettes de sang
Et si je creuse des orbites dans le globe séminal
De ta chair

Shadow of My Madness

If I eat flesh
If I tear your eyelids with my hands
If I eat the brain of my enemy
Vanquished
If I trap my pubis with rotten toothed rats
It is not to avenge myself
My river flows freely
My foundry overpopulated with blind artisans
Only once blew to kindle your passion
My dreams only tremble in the eyes of crocodiles
Love is only the issue of the host
Pulled from the ground
Mud smeared and still
Gesturing
My enemies my enemy my lover go
Feasting
Dancing on the tomb of my buried belly
A boardwalk
A palisade of trunks
A forest a giant egg
A tree
A mast with heavy sails lower
Than the horizon seen from the front when the moon no
        longer recedes
Everything rocks
One month one simple month separates me from this other
        greenery
My hatred is divided into sobs in droplets of blood
And if I dig circles in the seminal globe

Si je me venge en gobant l'oiseau-poisson
Encore vierge dans sa coquille
Si je macule ma couche
Si je hurle ton nom entre mes mâchoires à jamais scellées
Par l'oubli
C'est que je sens couler ton sperme dans mes narines
        encore soutenues
Par les ressorts de la longue nuit
Me réveillerai-je en sursaut
Trop tard
J'ai bu ta vie en trente nuits de rage
Nul ne peut défaire le mal qu'il fait en songe
Que de larmes dans ma nuit profonde

Of your flesh
If I get revenge by gobbling the bird-fish
Still a virgin in its shell
If I stain my diaper
If I throw your name between my jaws forever sealed
By oblivion
It is because I feel your sperm flowing in my nostrils still
        held up
By the coils of the long night
I will wake with a start
Too late
I drank your life in thirty nights of rage
No one can undo the hurt he does in dreams
None but the tears in my nightly depths

Le grand jamais

La roue cesse de tourner
Tourne encore
Rires perpétuels des faiseuses de pluie
Le noir centrifuge éclate sur le papier
Telle l'ombre venue de la forêt
L'image peureuse amorce un pas dans la clairière
Signe visible de la grenouille
Dans le vide vécu
L'écorce fond l'après-midi
L'aile du voyageur vogue à la dérive
Voilà l'eau de l'aquarelle
L'itinéraire du rêve dirigé au crayon
Labyrinthes de marbre
Silhouettes instables
Plages de silence flottant comme une ivresse
Celui qui voit éclaire

The Great Never

The wheel stops turning
Turns again
Perpetual laughter of rainmakers
Centrifugal black bursts appear on the page
Like the shadow from the forest
The fearful image steps into the clearing
Visible sign of the frog
In the lived void
Bark melts in the afternoon
The traveler's wing drifts
Here is the water of the watercolor
The dream's route sketched in pencil
Marble labyrinths
Unstable silhouettes
Beaches of silence floating like drunkenness
He who sees enlightens

Voici Juin

L'herbe éclate dans ma tête
Et une boule de feu en pâquerette
S'éternise
La vérité vêtue de mille vipères
Descend les marches de la colère sans trébucher
Rouge elle scintille au cœur du genêt brutal
Seul vous rêvez de venaison
De vos yeux de votre bouche sort le bel aujourd'hui
Mais votre retour n'est plus guère que celui du courrier
Et mon amour ballotté par des vagues contraires
Touche son crâne du bout de l'index indicateur
Pourquoi arracher le feu du ciel impalpable
Quand en moi il germe et fulmine
Pourquoi jeter son gant dans la foule
Demain est un moignon livide

Here Is June

Grass erupts in my head
And a daisy fireball
Drags on
The truth dressed in a thousand vipers
Descends the angry stairs without tripping
Red she sparkles at the heart of the brutal broom plant
Only you dream of venison
From your eyes from your mouth comes the beautiful today
But your return is nothing more than that of the mailman
And my love tossed about by contradictory waves
Touch his skull with the tip of your index finger
Why tear fire from the impalpable sky
When it already grows and smolders in me
Why throw your glove into the crowd
Tomorrow is a livid stump

Inventaire non exhaustif de l'indécent ou le nez de la méduse

Ce qui est indécent fait rougir
Le sang à la tête
Le choc en retour
La fuite en avant
Censure
Indécent le cercueil couvert d'un drapeau
Indécents les discours les médailles les morts au champ
d'honneur
Obscène la guerre
Indécente la solitude du vieillard
Obscène la misère
Indécent le paravent qui dérobe l'agonisant
Aux yeux des moribonds
Indécents les indifférents les béni-oui-oui les staliniens
Indécents les fascinés de l'Ordre
Les porteurs de matraque et de goupillon
Indécent le pas cadencé
La peine capitale la prison préventive
Indécents les asiles
Obscène la torture
Indécente la force armée
Qui se déploie sur les pavés de la ville en fête
Indécente l'acné roue de la boutonnière
Tout est légion sauf l'honneur
Indécente l'Académie ?
Trop d'honneur(s) !
Indécents ceux qui font parler les morts
La bouche enfarinée

Inexhaustive Inventory of the Indecent or Medusa's Nose

Indecency makes one blush
Blood rushes to the head
Backlash
Rushing ahead
Censorship
Indecent the coffin covered with a flag
Indecent the speeches the medals the dead on the field
of honor
Obscene war
Indecent the old man's loneliness
Obscene misery
Indecent the curtain that hides the dying
From the eyes of those close to death
Indecent the indifferents the yes-men the Stalinists
Indecent those fascinated by Order
The wearers of batons and aspergillum
Indecent the quick step
Capital punishment preventative prison
Indecent asylums
Obscene torture
Indecent armed forces
Who deploy on the cobblestones of the celebrating city
Indecent red boutonniere acne
Everything is legion except honor
Indecent Academy?
Too many award(s)!
Indecent those who make the dead speak
The floury mouth

Indécents les sondages de rein de la population passive
Indécent le bâillon
Obscène le baïonné
Indécent le racisme
Obscène la mort

Indecent the kidney catheterization of the passive
population
Indecent the gag
Obscene the gagged
Indecent racism
Obscene death

Pierre Molinier ou celui qui désire

Les méduses broutent debout
Somnolentes
Leurs doigts plongés dans la haute laine
Du frisson
Leurs yeux caillent derrière les rideaux de perles
Brouillant les pistes du pinceau Le printemps
Au niveau de la cavité buccale
L'hormone équiline galope sur la frise
D'un pubis frais rasé du matin
Une vraie Sainte-Chapelle sans anus ni épée
Tel un rire cascadeur
Une clarté louche tombe CRESCENDO
De sa rosace-spatangide
Sur les orgasmes d'Orient et les banquettes du vestibule
De l'Atelier du Grenier Saint Pierre
L'homme au béret mousseux comme un après-midi de
juillet
Écoute craquer les ténèbres ainsi que de vieux boisages
Il voit
Les chairs vénéneuses de son pulpeux fétiche
Les œufs papaux les étoiles malignes
Les dédales sonores de ses nuits blanches
Musardant sous les jupes ombellifères de
Celle-qui-se-penche
Sous les lambrequins ondoyants
Sous le sorbier et l'aubépine
De ses hanches
Il comprend
Le sauvage abandon de la convulsive écartelée

Pierre Molinier or One Who Desires

Jellyfish graze standing
Sleepily
Their fingers plunged in the high wool
Of the thrill
Their eyes curdle behind pearl curtains
Blurring the strokes of paintbrush Spring
In the oral cavity
The equiline hormone gallops on the frieze
Of a freshly shaven pubis in the morning
A real Sainte-Chapelle without anus or sword
Like a fake laugh
A shady clarity falls CRESCENDO
From the rosette heart urchin
On the orgasms of the Orient and the benches of the hall
From the Atelier du Grenier Saint Pierre
The man in a sparkling beret like an afternoon in July
Hears the darkness crack like old woodwork
He sees
The venomous flesh of her pulpy fetish
The papal eggs the malignant stars
The sonic mazes of his sleepless nights
Dawdling under the umbelliferous skirts of she-who-leans
Under the undulating mantling
Under the mountain ash and the hawthorn
Of her hips
He understands
The wild abandonment of the quartered convulsive
Between navel-less sleep and striking silk stockings
And the bone barometer of the chrysalis penis

Entre le sommeil sans nombril aux beaux bas de soie
Et le baromètre osseux du pénis chrysalide
Ensablées les larges cicatrices vicieuses
Zébrures sur le fond d'une autre nuit
Il sait
Que la voie royale du sexe reste
La haine

Sanded the wide vicious scars
Stripes on the background of another night
He knows
That the royal path of sex remains
Hatred

J'ai aimé un homme saturé de lui-même

Je te verrai plus tard
Sablonneuse enfant
Les flammes criardes de ma noir toison
Grésillent et tombent au moindre frisson
De l'air
L'interminable géranium croasse entre les pavés
Nue la peau du vivant cigare
Craquelle sous mes dents et son saignant prépuce
Erre
Va repose-toi enfant de mes vingt ans
Inflammable comme l'été dans les buissons stériles
Je veux suivre le brûlot de tes rêveries impubères
Revoir l'arène de ma première grande défaite
Rager sans m'éteindre sous un tas de cendres fines
Et boire la mort infâme sur mes lèvres autrefois

I Loved a Man Saturated with Himself

Later I will see you
Sandy child
The screaming flames of my black sheep fleece
Sizzle and fall at the slightest shiver
Of the air
The interminable geranium croaks between cobblestones
Bare the skin of the living cigar
Crackle under my teeth and his bleeding foreskin
Wander
Go rest child of my twenty years
Incendiary like summer in the barren bushes
I want to follow the fire of your prepubescent daydreams
Revisit the arena of my first great defeat
Rage without losing my flame beneath a pile of ash
And taste infamous death on my lips once more

Incendies spontanés

La nuit le ciel est un sexe ouvert
Le feu s'assoupit l'eau oisive se meurt
Le corps perd ses forces bien avant minuit
Désirant se voir mort il meurt déjà
Le temps n'est plus qu'un caveau funèbre
Pour celui qui halète dans la superstition
Les cadavres se souviennent de la mort
Longtemps après les quarante jours d'usage
La poussière n'étouffe que le déjà oublié
Les morts respirent
Le regard troué
La bouche étirée par le jeu électrique
De l'immense bâillement
De l'éternuement final
Par l'aspiration et le sanglot
Par le hoquet et le dernier rot
Si l'amour est le fils de l'œil
Le feu fils de bois
Et le vent fils du vide
Même les forêts peuvent espérer le brûlot
Y a-t-il douleur plus amoureuse de son aiguillon
Que la mienne
Le vinaigre ravive les blessures anciennes
L'insomnie aiguise les branches de l'étoile
Un souffle trop brusque et elle s'évapore
Si Dieu est un cerf-volant
Qui diable est George Sand

Spontaneous Combustion

At night the sky is an open sex
The fire dozes standing water dries
The body loses its strength long before midnight
Wishing to see himself dead he is already dying
Time is no more than a funeral vault
For he who gasps with superstition
Corpses remember death
Long after forty days of use
Dust only suffocates those already forgotten
The dead breathe
The pierced gaze
The mouth stretched by the electrical game
Of a huge yawn
Of the final sneeze
By breath and sob
By hiccups and the last burp
If love is the son of the eye
Then flame is the son of wood
And wind the son of emptiness
Even forests can hope for fire
Is there pain more in love with its sting
Than mine
Vinegar revives old wounds
Insomnia sharpens the star's points
Breathe too quickly and it evaporates
If God is a kite
Who the hell is George Sand

Le rire en rut

Le rire en rut
Dévale
Les pentes du cratère
Embolie
Le râle en rafales
Démolit
L'estocade contre l'insomnie
L'angoisse souffle comme le vent du Nord
Sur les plages de varech
Sur les champs de jonquilles
Semant des fils d'argent
Sur le crâne de veilleur égueulé
Comme un volcan
Et la vie ce reptile à coquille
S'accumule dans la vase
Tel l'azur annexé
Par le globe oculaire d'un batracien
Amok parmi les têtards

Laughter in Heat

Laughter in heat
Careens down
The slopes of the crater
Embolism
The death rattle's gusts
Demolish
The thrust against insomnia
Anguish blows like the North Wind
Over kelp beaches
Over daffodil fields
Sowing silver threads
On the skull of the open-mouthed watchman
Like a volcano
And life this shelled reptile
Accumulates in the mud
Like the azure annexed
By the eyeball of an amphibian
Running amok among the tadpoles

De l'impudeur jusque dans les aliments

Abel
L'homme aux seins opprimés
Le premier mort
Le mieux aimé
Celui qui sema la poussière
Dans la tombe de son père chrysalide Abel
Feu sucré du phallus dans la bouche même de l'orage
Celui qui souffla sa vie dans le gosier
De la nuit bitumeuse Frère
Tu es celui qui inventa l'ombre avant de connaître la
 lumière
Homme aux seins lourds et pâle sperme glacé
Lucifer
Celui qui mourut vierge
En rêvant toutes les guerres
Abel aux dents sonores
Et urine galipot
Je maudis ta faiblesse
Ta voix de Vénus callipyge
Tes exagérations intentionnelles
Tes jouissances fictives
Un jour tu dévisseras la mamelle
Qui suinte si doucement
La mort
Dans la gorge des étrangers
Tu arracheras les yeux pierreux
De la tombe où ils pâlissent
Dans le roulis
Du souvenir

From Shamelessness Even in Food

Abel
The man with oppressed breasts
The first death
The best loved
He who sowed the dust
In the tomb of his chrysalis father Abel
Sweet fire of the phallus in the storm's very mouth
The one who blew his life down the gullet
Of the bituminous night Brother
You are the one who invented shadow before knowing the
light
Man with heavy breasts and pale icy sperm
Lucifer
He who died a virgin
Dreaming of every war
Abel with sonorous teeth
And resinous urine
I curse your weakness
Your voice like the Callipygian Venus
Your intentional exaggerations
Your fake orgasms
One day you will unscrew the udder
That oozes death
So softly
Down the throats of strangers
You'll gouge out your stonelike eyes
From the grave where they wither
In the bobbing
Of memory

De ton poing fermé de ta langue au besoin
Tu scelleras l'anus de la terre boueuse
Cloaque béant aux sanglots de cratère
Tu chargeras
Et la mort mangera seule enfin

From your clenched fist from your language if necessary
You will seal the anus of the muddy earth
Gaping cesspool with crater's sobs
You will charge
And death will eat alone at last

Le crane écran du souvenir

L'œil dort comme une huître au fond de la baie
L'image souffre sous ses voiles mouillés
Sans entendre le roulement en vrille
Des pesants talismans
Qui
        sonnent
                l'heure
Sans arracher la tunique érotique
De la grande myope
Imaginaire
Sans ciller
L'œil parle et la ville prend feu
L'eau trouble aspire
Les rues sombrent
La flamme charbonneuse de l'alcool
Vacille dans le creux du regard
ABSENT
Le reflet grince des dents dans la glace
L'œil se fige
Qui connaît le visage de celui qui le précède
Sur le pont vagabond de la folie centrifuge
Le cochon velu mange la perle

The Skull Screen of Memory

The eye sleeps like an oyster in the depths of the bay
The image writhes beneath wet veils
Without hearing the spiraling roll
Of heavy talismans
That
          toll
                the hour
Without tearing off the erotic tunic
Of the great myope
Imaginary
Without blinking
The eye speaks and the town catches fire
Murky water inhales
The streets sink
The smoky flame of alcohol
Waves from the hollow gaze
ABSENT
The reflection grinds its teeth in the mirror
The eye freezes
Who knows the face of the one who precedes him
On the wandering bridge of centrifugal madness
The hairy pig eats the pearl

Il faut acheter son cercueil...

Il faut acheter son cercueil de son vivant
Le remplir n'est rien
Les grands yeux blancs du Solitaire y pourvoiront
Celui qui porte sa langue raidie
En fer de lance
Celui qui frappe le ciel et ses séjours
De sa colère d'enfant
Il faut laisser rôder sa rage
Entre les colonnes de Cartagena
L'Ancêtre reviendra sur ses béquilles d'airain
Semer des graines de cailloux
Entre les dents de porcelaine
Enfin libre du joug de la langue maternelle
Dans une famille de plusieurs frères
Le premier qui s'accouple expire
Tels ces blocs de granit qui font saillie hors de la terre
Dans les espaces trouble de la lande
Le pubis est un rocher qui sonne creux
Au matin
L'angoisse se nourrit de boue

You Must Buy Your Coffin...

You must buy your coffin while alive
Filling it is nothing
Solitaire's large white eyes will provide
For he who wears his stiff tongue
Spearhead
He who pounds the sky and its visits
With childish anger
You must let your rage lurk
Between the columns of Cartagena
The Ancestor will return on his brazen crutches
Sowing pebble seeds
Between porcelain teeth
Finally free from the yoke of the mother tongue
In a family of several brothers
The first to mate expires
Like the blocks of granite that jut from the ground
In the troubled spaces of the moor
The pubis is a rock that sounds hollow
In the morning
Anguish feeds on mud

Caresser une plaie

Caresser une plaie
Une très ancienne blessure
Baiser ses lèvres d'une langue d'orties
S'emparer de la douleur
Sortie saignante comme une mariée
De l'abattoir
Ratisser les allées de la rancune
De ses ongles retournés
Cracher son sperme dans la gueule ouverte du tombeau
Comme autant de cailloux gris
Mitraillés sur la grève
Marée montante du souvenir
Fouetter le sang frais
Battre le beurre
Pain d'aspics
Bouches meurtries
Rouler le roc qui annonce l'hystérie
Dans la gorge ensablée
De sa haine
Tousser arracher ses poumons
Pétale après pétale
Sangsuer la mort sur son lit vertigo
Ouïr l'éblouissement jaune
Du cri
Dans le silence de la terre obscure
J'entends pleurer les morts

Caress a Wound

Caress a wound
A very old wound
Kiss its lips with a tongue of nettles
Take hold of the pain
Leave bleeding like a bride
From a slaughterhouse
Raking the alleys of resentment
With her upturned nails
Spitting sperm into the tomb's open mouth
Like so many gray stones
Gunned down on the shore
Tide of memory rising
Whip fresh blood
Beat the butter
Aspic bread
Bruised mouths
Roll the rock that announces hysteria
Into the sandy throat
Of her hatred
Cough rip out the lungs
Petal by petal
Leech death on its vertigo bed
Hear the cry's
Yellow glare
In the silence of the dark earth
I hear the dead cry

Clarté au-delà du ressac

La mer clapote dans l'oreille de la plage endormie
Proie suintante de l'algue oisive
Le ciel sonne creux comme un roc
Au réveil
Des petites vagues chuchotent et se dandinent
Dans une coupe plus vaste que les parois
De l'horizon
L'arche de Noé brise ses côtes dur la digue
La nuit est favorable aux nageurs qui prennent le large
À la poursuite du sillon qui s'enfuit
Seuls surnagent
Deux chevaux morts
Et le jouet-androgyne
Ils chassent à courre
Sur les crêtes ponctuelles bleu de plomb
Tandis qui dans les allées moroses
Du profond minuit
La lune se pourlèche les babines

Clarity Beyond the Surf

The sea laps the beach's sleeping ear
Oozing lazy seaweed prey
The sky rings hollow like a rock
Upon waking
Little waves whisper and waddle
In a glass vaster than the walls
Of the horizon
Noah's ark breaks its ribs on the dam
Night is favorable for swimmers who prefer the open sea
Chasing the fleeing furrow
Two dead horses
Float alone
And the androgynous toy
They hunt
On the pointy leaden blue crests
While in the morose alleys
Of deepest midnight
The moon licks its chops

Mille gorges hurlent ensemble

Mille gorges hurlent ensemble
Dans les marges et ruelles
D'une tête inerte
Mille gorges hurlent ensemble
Sans fêlure sans bruit car
Un bâillon de sang
Fait cadenas
Mieux vaut en rire
Des bulles pourpres d'incendie
Moulantes comme la douleur
Seins soleil d'Odessa
Éruptions
Fin de nuit
La mort tire son bas de soie
Sur la face retroussée
Bleue verte et livide
Gomme les traits
De l'ami
Mille gorges brûlent ensemble
Toutes voix éteintes
Leurs langues mélangées
Cloquent
C'est la nuit pull-over

A Thousand Throats Howl Together

A thousand throats howl together
In the margins and alleys
Of a sluggish mind
A thousand throats howl together
Without cracks without noise because
A gag of blood
Makes a padlock
It is better to laugh
Purple bubbles of flame
Molded like pain
Odessa's sun-breasts
Erupt
Late night
Death pulls its silk stocking
On the upturned face
Blue green and livid
Erases the features
Of the friend
A thousand throats burn together
All voices go out
Their mixed tongues
Covered over
Night acts a sweater

The Great Never

(*Le grand jamais*, 1981)

Avez-vous lu ?
Avez-vous écrit ?
Avez-vous lu ce que vous avez écrit ?
Qui êtes-vous ?
Et surtout
Qu'attendez-vous de la gomme ?

J'ai aimé
J'ai tué
J'ai aimé celui qui s'est tu
Post-scriptum au Caire
Après tout
La transe suit le carnage
Comme l'œillet l'ordure
Qui savoure les cerises du lion flagada ?

Lorsque la foule reflue
La moule portant perle
Fait place à un animal sans testicules
Limaçon en armure d'écolier
Armée de génitalia en déroute

Ces hommes vendent cher leur blanc de baleine
Bougies de veille
Bougies de procession
Bougies sans flammes pour nuit de noces sur la lande
Bougies écumantes de la vieillesse enragée
Laissez chanter les beaux cétacés
Sur les hauts-fonds des villes
Dérivent les solitaires
Une goutte de sperme dans l'embouchure du métro
Et la peur ovipare fera raz-de-marée
Où sont les goulus de mer ?

Have you read?
Have you written?
Have you read what you have written?
Who are you?
And above all
What do you expect of the eraser?

I have loved
I have killed
I have loved the one who was quiet
Postscript in Cairo
After everything
The trance follows carnage
Like the carnation the garbage
Who savors the cherries of *Slap Happy Lion*?

When the swarm subsides
The clam with its pearl
Makes room for an animal without testicles
Snail in schoolboy armor
Army of genitalia in disarray

These men sell their whale blubber for a high price
Candles for vigils
Candles for processions
Candles without flames for wedding nights on the moor
Candles foaming with raging old age
Let the pretty porpoises sing
On the shoals of the city
Drift the lonely
A drop of sperm in the mouth of the metro
And oviparous fear will cause a tidal wave
Where are the gluttons of the sea?

Scalpé celui qui ne sait pas pleurer
Scalpés les enfants qui urinent sans attendre
Scalpés les romanciers qui se pressent au laminoir
Du hasard qui fait trop bien les choses
Qui veut boire son soûl sur le radeau de *la Méduse*
Que cache la petite main plantée dans le terreau
D'un vase de nuit ?
Scalpé celui qui saura dire : j'ai dû rêver à l'aube du
dernier jour
Son crâne sera gaine de torture

Si le cheval est la partie du nomade
La mouche le paravent d'aveugle
Et le sein la cible du cancer
La guerre n'est que rêve de fusil
Le mucus de la tombe irrigue les champs
Du sommeil sauvage
Une nuit longue comme l'hiver pour un écorché
Sur la banquise
Le dressage des chiens à fistule
Ne saurait surprendre la mort sur son perchoir
Elle chevauche le vent fort de ses menstrues
L'aigle disparaît le raisonnement fuit
Qui connaît la souffrance de cailloux ?

Étrange bal où l'on ne danse point
Niez le vampire la pieuvre apparaît
Les rares déguisés sans bec à goitre
Et masque de velours
Traquent l'amour sous la paupière retombée
Exercice de tristesse
Le Pays Basque en septembre
Les écailles se resserrent
Le cœur se déplace

Scalped the one who doesn't know how to cry
Scalped children who pee without waiting
Scalped novelists who rush to the press
Chance does things too well
Who wants to drink his fill on Medusa's raft
What hides the small planted hand in the soil
Of a night vase?
Scalped the one who would say: I must have dreamed at
    dawn of the last day
His head will be a torture sheath

If the horse is part of the nomad
The fly is a blind man's screen
And the breast the target of cancer
War is only the dream of a gun
The mucus of the tomb irrigates the fields
Of wild sleep
A night long as winter for a flayed man
On an iceberg
Training dogs with fistula
Cannot surprise death on its perch
She rides the wind of her menstrual flow
The eagle evaporates reason flees
Who can know the stone's suffering?

Strange ball where no one dances
Deny the vampire the octopus appears
The rare disguises without a goiter beak
And velvet mask
Stalk love beneath the fallen eyelid
Sad exercise
The Basque Country in September
The scales tighten
The heart moves

Lentement
Comme une truite au soleil
Sur le fond rocheux de la vie quotidienne
Évitez de marcher dans l'eau électrique
Fin du secteur souvenirs

L'engoulevent et le nain
Habitants de banlieue
Buveurs d'éther brûlant et clair
Courent les rues en costumes délétères
Le loup le vent la froidure
Singuliers voyageurs du dernier crâne empli de sang
Happent le sein fugace
Passent sans musique au gré des mâchoires
La peur tient le haut du pavé

Après la mort
La mouche à viande
Mange à sa faim
Dans le sillage de l'égout
Le pain des pissotières
Fleurit
Après l'assaut l'armée en déroute
Rampe vers les tranchées
Ouvertes sur la Grande Nuit
Seins béants bouches avides
Saignées nourricières
Plongées et remontées des têtards
Entre tripes et boyaux
Drapeaux en berne
Les yeux pleins du soleil levant
Verse du vin pour la mère

Slowly
Like a trout in the sun
On the rocky bottom of daily life
Avoid walking in electrified water
Edge of the memory sector

The nightjars and the dwarfs
Suburban dwellers
Ether drinkers burning and clear
Run the streets in injurious costumes
The wolf the wind the cold
Singular travelers of the last blood-filled skull
They grab the fleeting breast
Pass without music at the whim of the jaws
Fear has the upper hand

After death
The blowfly
Eats its fill
In the sewer's wake
Public toilet pastry
Blooms
After the assault the rerouted army
Crawls toward the trenches
Open on the Great Night
Gaping breasts eager mouths
Bloodied nourishers
The diving and surfacing of tadpoles
Between guts and bowels
Flags at half-mast
Eyes full of the rising sun
Pour wine for the mother

Folie pour folie
Il faut les marier
Le vase empli de vase
L'ovaire troué
La voix du poignard PERCE
L'œil du tremplin RIGIDE
(Vrai ou faux
Temps illimité)

Sur mon lit en béton armé
On y tue en abondance mais le meurtre n'est pas sanglant
Mon torse est un couvercle de cercueil
Femme virile ou homme voilé
Je déteste un être cher
Caractère magique de la défécation
Délivrance par l'écriture
Couper sa langue afin de châtrer le devin
Un coup de dent dans la bouffissure
Et c'en est fini de l'obsession
Si l'avenir de la folie est dans la couche du médecin

Enfouir les yeux dans une termitière
Enterrer les uns enferrer les autres
Introduire une mante dans l'orifice anal
Moudre les grains de beauté afin de brouiller leur écriture
Couver les œufs d'ennemi
Écraser les embryons
Danser sur le fil des années de plomb
Le rat rêve toujours sous son casque d'électrodes
Pas l'homme

Retirer ses lèvres de la couche immobile
Couvrir les miroirs de crêpe
Laisser partir le paquet tremblant *La tignas*

Madness for madness
You must marry them
The vase filled with vase
The perforated ovary
The dagger's voice PIERCES
The eye of the springboard TENSES
(True or false
Unlimited time)

On my reinforced concrete bed
There are plenty of deaths but the murder is not bloody
My chest is a coffin lid
Virile woman or veiled man
I hate a loved one
Magic character of defecation
Deliverance through writing
Cut out its tongue to castrate the psychic
A bite in the swelling
And the obsession is over
If the future of madness is in the doctor's mouth

Bury the eyes in a termite mound
Bury some sending others to hell
Introduce a mantis into the anal orifice
Grind beauty marks to blur their writing
Cover the enemies' eggs
Crush the embryos
Dance on the wire of leaden years
The rat dreams constantly under its electrode helmet
Not the man

Remove your lips from the immobile layer
Cover the mirrors with fabric
Let go of the trembling package *La tignas*

Sans hâte ni bigoudis
Ne plus essuyer la morve des babines
La langue érodée des mourants
Sombre sans écho
À quoi bon téter le sein de la famille
Quand le râle éteint
Les yeux renversés
L'enveloppe vide repose jambes écartées
L'horreur se nomme de tout son long
Le repas de la vie est terminé
À quoi bon les bottelettes
Les sermons les vidanges
Les yeux fripés
Seules les dents vont
Déchaussées
Sur le tapis roulant de la mort

Un cheval borgne s'emballe
Folie équestre ou démarche officielle
Du temps dans la nuit tombale
Une ligne tirée du centre au milieu d'arc
Saigne le cadran caché
Dans l'entresol le temps passe comme il peut
Meule rapide pieds plats ou talons aiguilles
La rage ravage le vent tonsure
Sur le ventre du désert
Un cheveu se fait pieu
Épingle comme un insecte sur un buvard
Une charogne chevaline
S'empale
Sillage du bal dans le chant de l'oiseau
Violence croissante de l'ennui
La sueur jaillit du mamelon
Comme du lai

Without haste or curlers
No more wiping snot from the muzzle
The worn tongue of the dying
Somber without echo
What good is it to suckle at the family breast
When the death rattle leaves
The upturned eyes
The empty envelope rests with splayed limbs
Horror had a name all along
The feast of life is over
What good are the bundles of flowers
The sermons the drains
The wrinkled eyes
Only the teeth go
Loose
On the conveyor of death

A one-eyed horse runs wild
Equestrian madness or official gait
Time in the falling night
A line drawn from the center to the middle of the arc
Bleeds the hidden dial
In the mezzanine time passes as it can
Quick-grinding flat feet or stilettos
Rage ravages the wind tonsures
The desert's stomach
A hair becomes a stake
Pinned like an insect to blotting paper
A horse carrion
Impales itself
Aftermath of the ball in birdsong
Growing violence of boredom
Sweat gushes from the nipple
Like milk

Ahanements des Levantins
Rires
Seuls les animaux à l'ongle fendu
Sont bons à manger
Les autres sont impurs
Heureux les pauvres d'esprit qui manipulent leurs
excréments
Solution mécanique du problème l'éventail
Qui connaît la valeur de l'argent ?

Kundalini bouge
Lourdement lové dans la graisse de l'esclavage
Elle ne fait que frémir depuis bientôt trop longtemps
Il faut murer les cimetières
Abolir les certitudes
Je n'entends plus pleurer derrière la cloison
Un enfant mourra demain
Des bribes des pensées d'autrui
Strient ma tête surchauffée
Comme des éclats de trompettes dans une énorme
tabagie
Apprendrai-je enfin à laisser passer le moment venu
Sans m'exposer au combat ?
Kundalini glisse anneau après année
Sur l'index rouillée de l'haruspicine
La ponte est finie reste la sanie du cadavre
Leitmotiv de fards sur le plafond de marais
Le serpent répond toujours à l'appel du l'oiseau

De Lundi à Samedi
La douleur sans tête
Éjacule son prurit
Dans le vide opiacé
Du mensonge

Panting Levantines
Laughing
Only animals with cloven hooves
Are good for eating
The others are impure
Blessed are the poor in spirit who handle their excrement
Mechanical solution for the fan problem
Who knows the value of money?

Kundalini moves
Heavily coiled in the grease of slavery
It's been shivering for too long now
We must wall up the cemeteries
Abolish certainties
I no longer hear crying behind the partition
A child will die tomorrow
Snippets of other people's thoughts
Stoke my overheated head
Like bursts of trumpet in a huge smoke shop
Will I finally learn to let the moment pass
Without exposing myself to combat?
Kundalini slips ring after ring
On the rusty index of the haruspex
The egg-laying is finished the sanity of the corpse remains
Leitmotif of blush on the swamp ceiling
The serpent always answers the bird's call

From Monday to Saturday
Headless pain
Squirts its irrepressible desire
In the opiate void
Of lies

Visages détournés
Baisers à la hâte
Flamme de mille crotales
Rayons de brume
De la boue jusqu'à l'horizon
La colère souffle en tempête
Dans l'anus de la nourrice
Gouttelettes de femme sur le pare-brise
Maladie profonde

De Lundi à Samedi
Dépravation rage et gloutonnerie
Haut-le-cœur devant l'image maternelle
Accroupie
Relents de cuisine dans les orties
Absences et ordure
De la Dame de la Salle du Suprême Jugement
Trombes de lait dans la bouche de l'avorton
Mort-né

Naître et croître près d'un grand fleuve
Sans boire de son eau
Cantique des damnés étouffés dans la boue
Côtoyer les ours blancs vendeurs d'aromates
Va-nu-pieds entre les lignes du destin
Sans chercher la plante sous la dalle
Ni le feuillage dans les yeux de cire
Vois sans comprendre souffrir sans apprendre
Aimer son prochain sans enterrer ses géniteurs
Voilà la houle des vivants sans fin ni commencement
Rêves prolongés de la mort

Averted faces
Hasty kisses
Flame of a thousand rattlesnakes
Rays of mist
From the mud to the horizon
Anger blows into a storm
In the nurse's anus
Woman droplets on the windshield
Deep sickness

From Monday to Saturday
Depravity rage and gluttony
Gagging in front of the maternal image
Crouched
Smells of cooking in the nettles
Absences and trash
Of the Lady of the Hall of Supreme Judgement
Showers of milk in the mouth of the runt
Stillborn

To be born and grow near a river
Without drinking its water
Song of the damned smothered in mud
Float along with polar bears sellers of herbs
Go barefoot between the lines of fate
Without looking for the plant beneath the slab
Nor foliage in the waxy eyes
See without understanding suffer without learning
Love your neighbor without burying your parents
Here is the swell of the living without beginning or end
Prolonged dreams of death

Jadis les amants
Ôtaient leur âme
Avant le combat

Pas besoin d'opium
Pas besoin d'hypnose
Un doigt d'acier dans l'iris
Et voilà le fantôme
En amont de l'amant
« Compris » dis Bob dans son petit lit roulant
Et il expire
Centaurée petite fleur
Elle guérit les chairs disjointes
Mais l'abcès éclata seul sur la plage
Comme en melon sous les roues
D'une dentition malpropre
Deux doigts décapuchonnés
Petits pélicans délicates tenailles
Trempèrent leur charpie
Dans la plaie inerte où gisent
Les cailloux du chemin
Douceur et torture de la seule certitude
Un jour prochain sous un monticule de flots
La solitude hurlante hurlera hurlera
L'ordre enfin
Tout ce que l'on fuit
Nomades

Et si la langue s'enroule autour du sexe
Comme le serpent autour de l'arbre
Phallus vivant sur bois mort
Pourquoi l'imaginaire ondule-t-il
Au rythme des mots
Dedans – dehors ?

Once the lovers
Removed their souls
Before the fight

No need for opium
No need for hypnosis
A steel finger in the iris
And the ghost appears
Upriver of the lover
"Understood" says Bob in his little cot
And he exhales
Small flower knapweed
It heals broken flesh
But the abscess burst alone on the beach
Like a melon under the tires
Of unclean teeth
Two uncovered fingers
Small pelicans delicate pinchers
Soak their lint
In the inert wound where
Stones of the path lie
Kindness and torture of the only certainty
One day soon beneath a mound of waves
Howling loneliness will howl and howl
Order at last
Everything we flee from
Nomads

And if the tongue wraps around the sex
Like a serpent around a tree
Living phallus on dead wood
Why does the imaginary undulate
To the rhythm of words
Inside—outside?

La femme trembla et les cieux suintèrent
Du sang du sperme et des crapauds transparents
Les montagnes de ses cuisses
Se fondirent en eaux
Le sommeil fit demi-tour
Beau soleil tiré de la pierre
Combattant la femme comme un adversaire
S'avançant au bruit des cymbales de l'aube
Du levant au couchant aux jours des équinoxes
La femme créa le chaos la vie et le désespoir
Comme la jalousie dans le ventre du cancer
Don Juan est un grand trou noir

Donnez-moi un morceau de charbon
J'en ferai un aveugle
Donnez-moi un crâne épars sur le parquet
J'en ferai une descente aux flambeaux
Dans la fosse des passions durables
Donnez-moi un château mammaire
Je plongerai tête-bêche riant au suicide
Dans la résille verte d'une nuit d'octobre
Donnez-moi un grain de poussière
J'en ferai une montagne de haine
Chancelante et grave un arcane
Pour vous enterrer
Donnez-moi une langue de haute laine
J'enseignerai aux seigneurs
Comment briser leurs dieux de craie
Leurs pénis édentés
Aux pieds du grand corbeau blanc
Pourcroâ ?

Sur la frontière du sommeil
Des grands arbres fantomatiques

The woman trembled and the skies oozed
With blood sperm and transparent toads
The mountains of her thighs
Melted into waters
Sleep turned around
Beautiful sun pulled from the stone
Fighting the woman like an adversary
Advancing the sound of dawn's cymbals
From sunrise to sunset on equinox days
The woman created chaos life and despair
Like jealousy in the belly of cancer
Don Juan is a big black hole

Give me a piece of coal
I'll make a blind man out of it
Give me a skull scattered on the floor
I will make it a beacon descending
Into the pit of lasting passion
Give me a mammary castle
I will plunge headlong laughing at suicide
Into the green hairnet of an October night
Give me a speck of dust
I will make it a mountain of hate
Tottering and carving a mystery
To bury you
Give me a high wool tongue
I will teach the masters
How to shatter their Gods of chalk
Their toothless penises
At the feet of a great white raven
Why?

At the border of sleep
Big ghostly trees

Laissent flotter leur chevelure
La nuit dans le désert
Les angoisses vieilles rengaines
Comme des sentinelles
Tirent sans avertissement
Semis d'aigulles sur cerveau à fond de verre
Je veux je veux je veux
Libérer ton bras droit
Faire craquer les jointures des montagnes sous la mer
Scruter les entrailles du faiseur de pluie
Être homme à mon heure
L'expérience de la neige a réussi ?
Belle mort pour une femme de science

Lavez vos yeux dans l'urine
Rincez vos bouches dans l'urine
Buvez l'urine de vos vaches sacrées
Dans la botte secrète
D'un cul-de-jatte
Oubliez l'Orient
C'est la vie
Le crépuscule s'étale comme des fesses sur un banc
Partout meurt le bel après-midi
Prenez le deuil mais pour rire
Une taupe éventrée souille le sentier de ses entrailles
Pas le rat
Animal d'ordre et de ricanement
Le rat crève debout
Face à l'oppresseur toutes dents dehors
Inutilement vorace dans la tourbe amollie
Le cadre de l'horizon s'estompe dans la brune
La mort brandit son boyau ridé
Devant la parte des matrices
C'est la vie

Let their hair float
Night in the desert
Old anguish returns
Like sentinels
Shoot without warning
Eagle seeds on a glass-bottomed brain
I want I want I want
To free your right arm
To crack the joints of undersea mountains
Scrutinize the insides of the rainmaker
To be a man in my time
Did the snow experiment work?
Beautiful death for a woman of science

Wash your eyes in urine
Rinse your mouths in urine
Drink the urine of your sacred cows
In the secret boot
Of a legless man
Forget the Orient
This is life
Twilight spreads like an ass on a bench
Everywhere the pretty afternoon dies
Mourn in order to laugh
A disemboweled mole stains the path with its innards
Not the rat
Animal of order and spite
The rat dies standing
Facing the oppressor with bared teeth
Uselessly voracious in the soft peat
The frame of the horizon fades into the dark
Death brandishes its wrinkled gut
Before the door of the wombs
This is life

Arrachez trois ongles au cadavre incarnés
Deux verrues
Un pied plat
Simulez une érection
Brizes l'hymen de la basse obstinée
Et revenez demain
Vaincu par l'insomnie
C'est la vie qui s'annonce
C'est la vie

Tant va la tête à l'eau
Les yeux vont se noyer
Dans l'oreiller cannibale
Tel est le sommeil
Compteur de solitudes
Course de rats dans les allées de l'utérus
À partir de la dune
L'idée fixe tourne en rond
Dressée sur ses ergots
À quoi servent les décorations
Les fleurs les fleurs les perforations
Une fois la langue tirée
Il faut la traire

Certaines idées superstitieuses
Circulent
D'autres prennent racine dans les couloirs de l'insomnie
Luther conseille la moquerie
Comme arme légère contre les spectres
Joe avait de l'humour mais sa mère n'en avait pas
Foutaises que tout cela dit-il
Et Honorine se laissa prendre par-derrière
Sans oublier les génuflexions d'usage
Le regard fixe

Tear three fingernails from the incarnated corpse
Two warts
A flat foot
Simulate an erection
Break the hymen of the stubborn low bass
And come back tomorrow
Vanquished by insomnia
It is life that announces
This is life

So much goes with the head into the water
The eyes are going to drown
In the cannibal pillow
This is sleep
Enumerator of solitudes
Rat race in the alleys of the womb
From the dune
The obsession turns in circles
Upright on its spurs
To what end are the decorations
The flowers the flowers the perforations
Once the tongue sticks out
You have to milk it

Certain superstitious ideas
Circulate
Others take root in insomnia's corridors
Luther advises mockery
As a light weapon against specters
Joe had a sense of humor but his mother didn't
That's all bullshit he said
And Honorine let herself be taken from behind
Without forgetting the customary genuflections
The fixed stare

L'ail et le sel répandus
Sur l'Image

Dans le ciel du soleil invisible
L'œil fulgurant saigne
Tournoie
Se révulse
Fait glouglou
Un œil couronné d'épines
Grand bol de sommeil limpide
Accroché comme une icône
À un clou
Une médaille monsieur l'abbé
Pour peser sur la paupière
Quand le parquet se fait mou
L'œil farouche
Clignote derrière la fontanelle
Arrachons-la comme une mauvaise dent
Mieux vaut être myope que voyant
Dans un monde de petits rongeurs

Garlic and salt sprinkled
On the Image

In the sky of the invisible sun
The dazzling eye bleeds
Turns
Revolves
Gurgles
An eye crowned with spines
Great bowl of limpid sleep
Hanging like an icon
On a nail
A medal Monsieur Abbot
To weigh on the eyelid
When the floor is wet
The fierce eye
Blinks behind the fontanel
Let's pull it out like a bad tooth
Better to be shortsighted than clairvoyant
In a world of little rodents

Translator's Note

IT SEEMS COMMON KNOWLEDGE THAT the French phrase *la petite mort*, or "the little death," refers to the experience of orgasm. No one makes this conflation of death and desire clearer than the poet Joyce Mansour, who animates these twin flames throughout her impressive oeuvre. A preeminent post-war Surrealist, her strange and ravenous work introduces us to a different type of Surrealism, one without the self-assured masculine voice that dominated the movement.

The more well-known masculine Surrealism's relationship to women was clearly articulated by André Breton when he created the *femme enfant*, or child woman, a trope in which women are both sexual and innocent, willing to fulfill male desire without challenge. Mansour refuses this impossible position completely, insisting instead on women's own powerful desires.

What draws me to Mansour again and again is the full emotional range she allows for women—from anger and despair to pleasure and eroticism. By engaging such taboos as cannibalism and incest, her poems unleash a feminism that cannot be contained within any school of thought. Mansour reanimates and radicalizes desire. She gives it back its teeth.

Mansour's poetics may be understood as products of her own exile and liminality: a woman from a Syrian-Jewish family whose first language was English and yet chose to write in French, and who was banished from her home in Egypt during the rise of Gamal Abdel Nasser. Her life experiences open the door to a poetics without imitation.

English-language translators and publishers have focused mostly on Mansour's early work. Single volumes such as *Cris* (1953), *Déchirures* (1955), and *Carré Blanc* (1965) were translated, respectively, as *Screams* (1992), *Torn Apart*

(1999), and *Flash Card* (1978). A volume of selected poems was published in 2008, and another appeared more recently, in 2022. All of these translations—except for the most recent selected (from City Lights)—are now out of print, as are most of her books in France. Mansour's publication history has placed her in a precarious position on the edge of obscurity. It seems, therefore, all the more important to bring the full range of her work into English.

This volume is the first to focus on her later work and draws from four books written between 1960 and 1977: *Rapaces* (*Birds of Prey*), 1960; *Carré Blanc* (*White Square*), 1965; *Les Damnations* (*The Damnations*), 1967; and *Faire Signe au Machiniste* (*To Signal the Machinist*), 1977. I have also included two long poems in their entirety: *Astres et Désastres* (*Cosmos and Catastrophe*), 1969, and *Le Grand Jamais* (*The Great Never*), 1981, both originally published in illustrated stand-alone editions with artwork by Pierre Alechinsky. (The second also featured work by Roberto Matta.)

Needless to say, the work of women artists is often overshadowed by their biographies: who they knew and married is often more widely known than what they painted or wrote. Similarly, critical assessments of Mansour's work hardly ever pass up the chance to mention Breton's appreciation of her poems. While Breton's friendship and championing of her work was clearly important to Mansour herself (both *White Square* and *The Damnations* were dedicated to him), this collection shows her growing in ever stranger directions after his death in 1966, suggesting that the father of Surrealism may have held her back as much as he propelled her forward.

As she aged, Mansour's preoccupations turned inward. When she developed breast cancer, her celebration of female violence and unending, nearly consumptive desire gained a metaphoric dimension. The body—her body—in which she took pleasure, and which she feared for its great erotic charge, began to eat away at her. This pushed her work in grimmer and more fearless directions. At times, her illness yielded turns toward more biographical writing. For instance, in *The Great Never*, she writes, "If the horse is part of the nomad / The fly is a blind man's screen / And the breast the target of cancer." Still, death is only a portal to someone's (or something's) desire: "After death / The blowfly / Eats its fill."

Thanks to her quotidian diction and spare syntax, translating Mansour is (deceptively) simple. The strange genius of her work appears in the juxtaposition of images and the subject matter itself. My aim is to recreate the experience of reading these poems in French, of amazement at the poet's ability to unite disparate images with seeming ease. I try to maintain this effect by replicating her relatively unpretentious language as directly as possible and letting the images speak.

Translators sometimes obsess over the quandary of domestication and foreignization. The former approach may assimilate a text in a way that erases difference, whereas the latter risks exoticizing the otherness of the original. While translating Mansour, I was faced with difficult choices in regard to these two poles. For example, in "Inexhaustive Inventory of the Indecent or Medusa's Nose" she writes, "Indécents les indifférents les béni-oui-oui les staliniens." *Béni-oui-oui* was a derogatory term for Muslims who collaborated with colonial authorities during French rule in North Africa, especially in Algeria and Morocco. Although my translation of the term ("yes-men") may elide this important history, I felt that leaving the original French phrase in italics would speak only to an exclusive readership. Mansour's intention, it seems to me, is not to narrow the audience of the poem, which also mentions Stalinists and can be read more broadly as a poem against totalitarianism.

While I often had to navigate between specific contexts and what seemed necessary to transmit to the reader, there is also a larger sense in which this quandary occupied me: I was faced with whether to domesticate or foreignize Mansour's very thought. Surrealism's investment in free association is by now notorious. As Breton wrote in the 1924 *Manifesto*, "Surrealism is based on the belief in the superior reality of certain forms of previously neglected associations, in the omnipotence of dream, in the disinterested play of thought." So, to translate Mansour, I had to interpret her dreamlike association well enough to translate a coherent poem—a sort of domestication—but also leave the wildness intact.

Inundated as we are in our times with visual stimuli, Mansour's images may still shock you. The intended effect of surprise or disgust has an important purpose: to pull the reader out of the everyday and reanimate the experience of life itself. The fact that Surrealism offers a bracing slap in the face can be linked to its emergence in a time of rising fascist and totalitarian forces. The movement's revival during our own politically turbulent era is evidenced by recent exhibits, such as the Metropolitan Museum's "Surrealism Beyond Borders" show. I hope that my reimagining of Mansour in English will lead those without access to the original French to join her in imagining a new world.

—C. Francis Fisher

Acknowledgements

First, I would like to thank Cyrille Mansour for his generosity with his mother's legacy. I would also like to thank the editor of World Poetry, Matvei Yankelevich, whose support of young translators makes our field a better place, and whose sharp eye was integral in the completion of this book. I'm thankful, too, for the hard work of World Poetry's publicist, James Loop. Thank you also to Jocelyn Spaar, Jake Syersak, and Ariel Courage for your careful, diligent edits.

Some of these translations have appeared in *Chicago Review*, *The Brooklyn Rail*, *New England Review*, and *Copper Nickel*. My thanks to the editors of these magazines for giving the poems a home.

Thank you to my teachers who made translation a possibility, Katrina Dodson and Susan Bernofsky. Thank you also to friends and classmates who read these poems in workshops. Thank you to my Francophone friends in Brussels, Stéphane Odribinski and Nina Vanspranghe, who were always willing to lend a helping hand.

A lifetime of thank yous to my family, who has always given me the space to pursue my interests. And thank you to Noah for being my first and most honest reader, and for making our life possible.

—*C.F.F.*

One of the most important female Surrealist writers, ***Joyce Mansour*** (1928–1986) was born in England to Syrian-Jewish parents. Soon after her birth, the family moved to Cairo, where Mansour lived until she was forced to emigrate. She settled in Paris in 1953, where she continued writing and became a key member of the postwar Surrealist milieu. Mansour published sixteen books of poetry in her lifetime as well as prose and theater pieces. She died of cancer in Paris in 1986.

C. Francis Fisher received her MFA in poetry from Columbia University. Her work has appeared in *The Brooklyn Rail*, *The Yale Review*, and *The Los Angeles Review of Books*, among others. She curates Colloquy, a New York City event series that provides a forum for translators to engage with live audiences in an exploration of the art of translation. *In the Glittering Maw* is her first book of translations.

Literary critic, translator, and art historian ***Mary Ann Caws*** has written widely on Surrealist poetry and art. She is the author of several biographies (Marcel Proust, Virginia Woolf, Henry James, Pablo Picasso, Salvador Dalí) and has translated Stéphane Mallarmé, Tristan Tzara, Pierre Reverdy, André Breton, Paul Éluard, Robert Desnos, and René Char. She is the editor of *Manifesto: A Century of Isms* and *The Yale Anthology of Twentieth-Century French Poetry*.

This book was typeset in GT Alpina, a contemporary serif designed by Reto Moser for Grilli Type. The artwork on the cover is by Pierre Alechinsky, a friend and collaborator of Joyce Mansour. (One of the poems in this collection, "Cosmos and Catastrophes," is dedicated to him.) Alechinsky's lithograph "Braises" (from 1977) is printed courtesy of the artist and Galerie Lelong & Co., Paris. Designed by Andrew Bourne, the cover features lettering based on Alechinsky's distinctive script. Typesetting by Don't Look Now. Printed and bound by BALTO Print in Lithuania.

Marie-Noëlle Agniau
The Escapades
tr. Jesse Hover Amar

Jean-Paul Auxeméry
Selected Poems
tr. Nathaniel Tarn

Boethius
The Poems from On the Consolation of Philosophy
tr. Peter Glassgold

Maria Borio
Transparencies
tr. Danielle Pieratti

Jeannette L. Clariond
Goddesses of Water
tr. Samantha Schnee

Jacques Darras
John Scotus Eriugena at Laon
tr. Richard Sieburth

Mario dell'Arco
Day Lasts Forever: Selected Poems
tr. Marc Alan Di Martino

Olivia Elias
Chaos, Crossing
tr. Kareem James Abu-Zeid

Jerzy Ficowski
Everything I Don't Know
tr. Jennifer Grotz & Piotr Sommer
PEN AWARD FOR POETRY IN TRANSLATION

Antonio Gamoneda
Book of the Cold
tr. Katherine M. Hedeen & Víctor Rodríguez Núñez

Mireille Gansel
Soul House
tr. Joan Seliger Sidney

Óscar García Sierra
Houston, I'm the problem
tr. Carmen Yus Quintero

Phoebe Giannisi
Homerica
tr. Brian Sneeden

Zuzanna Ginczanka
On Centaurs & Other Poems
tr. Alex Braslavsky

Julien Gracq
Abounding Freedom
tr. Alice Yang

Leeladhar Jagoori
What of the Earth Was Saved
tr. Matt Reeck

Nakedness Is My End: Poems from the Greek Anthology
tr. Edmund Keeley

Jazra Khaleed
The Light That Burns Us
ed. Karen Van Dyck

Judith Kiros
O
tr. Kira Josefsson

Dimitra Kotoula
The Slow Horizon That Breathes
tr. Maria Nazos

Maria Laina
Hers
tr. Karen Van Dyck

Maria Laina
Rose Fear
tr. Sarah McCann

Perrin Langda
A Few Microseconds on Earth
tr. Pauline Levy Valensi

Afrizal Malna
Document Shredding Museum
tr. Daniel Owen

Joyce Mansour
In the Glittering Maw: Selected Poems
tr. C. Francis Fisher

Manuel Maples Arce
Stridentist Poems
tr. KM Cascia

Ennio Moltedo
Night
tr. Marguerite Feitlowitz

Meret Oppenheim
The Loveliest Vowel Empties: Collected Poems
tr. Kathleen Heil

Giovanni Pascoli
Last Dream
tr. Geoffrey Brock
RAIZISS/DE PALCHI TRANSLATION AWARD

Gabriel Pomerand
Saint Ghetto of the Loans
tr. Michael Kasper & Bhamati Viswanathan

Rainer Maria Rilke
Where the Paths Do Not Go
tr. Burton Pike

Elisabeth Rynell
Night Talks
tr. Rika Lesser

Waly Salomão
Border Fare
tr. Maryam Monalisa Gharavi

George Sarantaris
Abyss and Song: Selected Poems
tr. Pria Louka

George Seferis
Book of Exercises II
tr. Jennifer R. Kellogg

Seo Jung Hak
The Cheapest France in Town
tr. Megan Sungyoon

Ardengo Soffici
Simultaneities & Lyric Chemisms
tr. Olivia E. Sears

Paul Verlaine
Before Wisdom: The Early Poems
tr. Keith Waldrop & K.A. Hays

Witold Wirpsza
Apotheosis of Music
tr. Frank L. Vigoda

Uljana Wolf
kochanie, today i bought bread
tr. Greg Nissan

Ye Lijun
My Mountain Country
tr. Fiona Sze-Lorrain

Verónica Zondek
Cold Fire
tr. Katherine Silver